Tourism and Architectural Simulacra

Since its beginnings, tourism has inspired built environments that have suggested reinvented relationships with their original architectural inspirations. Copies, reinterpretations, and simulacra still constitute some of the most familiar and popular tourist attractions in the world.

Some reinterpret archetypes such as the ancient palace, the Renaissance villa, or the Mediterranean village. Others duplicate the cities in which we lived in the past or we still live today. And others realise perceptions of utopias such as Shangri-La, Eden, or Paradise. Replicas – duplitecture – and simulacra can have symbolic meaning for tourists, as merely inspiring an atmosphere or as truly authentic, and their relationship to original functions, for worship, accommodation, leisure, or shopping.

Tourism and Architectural Simulacra questions and rethinks the different environments constructed or adapted both for and by tourism exploring the relationship between the architectural inspiration and its reproduction within the tourist bubble. The wide range of geographical areas, eras, and subjects in this book show that the expositions of simulacra and hyper reality by Baudrillard, Deleuze, and Eco are surpassed by our complex world. Adopting an interdisciplinary approach they offer original insights of the complex relationship between tourism and architecture.

The chapters in this book were originally published as a special issue of the *Journal of Tourism and Cultural Change*.

Nelson Graburn was educated at Cambridge (1958), McGill (1960), and Chicago (PhD, 1963). He has taught at UC Berkeley for 54 years and served as Curator of the Hearst Museum and chair of Tourism Studies. He also taught in Canada, France, UK, Japan, and Brazil and China, and researched Canadian Inuit (1959–2014), Japan (since 1974), and China (since 1991). His work includes *Ethnic and Tourist Arts* (1976), *Japanese Domestic Tourism* (1983), *Anthropology of Tourism* (1983), *Multiculturalism in the New Japan* (2008), *Anthropology in the Age of Tourism* (2009), *Tourism and Glocalization* (2010), *Tourism Imaginaries: Anthropological Approaches* (2014), *Tourism Imaginaries at the Disciplinary Crossroads* (2016), *Tourism in (Post)Socialist Eastern Europe* (2017), and *Cultural Tourism Movements* (2018).

Maria Gravari-Barbas has a degree in Architecture and Urban Design (University of Athens, 1985) and a PhD in Geography and Planning (Paris IV – Sorbonne, 1991). She was Fellow at the Urban Program of Johns Hopkins University, Baltimore, USA (1990). She is the director of the EIREST, a multidisciplinary research team dedicated to tourism studies, with main focus on cultural heritage, development, and urban-tourism evolutions. From 2008 to 2017 she was the director of the Institute for Research and High Studies on Tourism (Institut de Recherches et d'Etudes Supérieures du Tourisme, IREST) of Paris 1 Panthéon-Sorbonne University. Since 2009 she is the director of the UNESCO Chair of Paris 1 Panthéon-Sorbonne University and the coordinator of the UNITWIN network 'Tourism, Culture, Development'. She is the author of several books and papers related to tourism, culture, and heritage.

Jean-François Staszak received his PhD in Geography at the Sorbonne University. After serving as Associate Professor in the Universities of Amiens (Northern France) and Panthéon-Sorbonne (Paris), he became full Professor at the Geography Department of the University of Geneva (Switzerland). His early research focused on the history and epistemology of Geography, and then on economic and cultural Geography. His most recent work addresses geographical imaginaries in the fields of art and tourism, analysing the geographical othering process and especially the exotic. His understanding of the articulation of geographical representations, practices, and realities owes much to deconstructionist theories and to postcolonial and gender studies. Among his recent books: *Quartier réservé. Bousbir, Casablanca Genève*, Georg (2020), *Simuler le monde. Panoramas, parcs à theme et autres dispositifs immersifs*, Genève, Métispresse (2019), *Frontières en tous genres. Cloisonnement spatial et constructions identitaires*, Rennes, PUR (2017), *Clichés exotiques. Le Tour du Monde en photographies 1860–1890*, Paris, De Monza (2015).

Tourism and Architectural Simulacra

Edited by
**Nelson Graburn, Maria Gravari-Barbas and
Jean-François Staszak**

LONDON AND NEW YORK

First published 2022
by Routledge
2 Park Square, Milton Park, Abingdon, Oxon OX14 4RN

and by Routledge
605 Third Avenue, New York, NY 10158

Routledge is an imprint of the Taylor & Francis Group, an informa business

British Library Cataloguing in Publication Data
A catalogue record for this book is available from the British Library

ISBN: 978-0-367-69456-2 (hbk)
ISBN: 978-0-367-69457-9 (pbk)
ISBN: 978-1-003-14188-4 (ebk)

Typeset in Myriad Pro
by Newgen Publishing UK

Publisher's Note
The publisher accepts responsibility for any inconsistencies that may have arisen during the conversion of this book from journal articles to book chapters, namely the inclusion of journal terminology.

Disclaimer
Every effort has been made to contact copyright holders for their permission to reprint material in this book. The publishers would be grateful to hear from any copyright holder who is not here acknowledged and will undertake to rectify any errors or omissions in future editions of this book.

Contents

Citation Information

The chapters in this book were originally published in the *Journal of Tourism and Cultural Change*, volume 17, issue 1 (2019). When citing this material, please use the original page numbering for each article, as follows:

Chapter 6

Chapter 7

For any permission-related enquiries please visit:
www.tandfonline.com/page/help/permissions

Notes on Contributors

Roberto Bartholo, Technology and Social Development Laboratory - LTDS, COPPE/Federal University of Rio de Janeiro - UFRJ, Rio de Janeiro, Brazil.

Bauer Bernhard, Consultant for socio-economic, cultural and tourism development, Vienna, Austria.

Yasmin Buchrieser, EIREST EA 7337, Université Paris I Panthéon-Sorbonne, Paris, France.

Canestrini Duccio, Sociology and Anthropology of Tourism, University Campus of Lucca, Pisa, Italy.

Bertram M. Gordon, Department of History, Mills College, Oakland, CA, USA.

Nelson Graburn, Department of Anthropology, University of Berkeley, Berkeley, CA, USA.

Maria Gravari-Barbas, IREST, EIREST, Paris 1 Panthéon-Sorbonne University, Paris, France.

Felipe Loureiro, Technology and Social Development Laboratory - LTDS, COPPE/Federal University of Rio de Janeiro - UFRJ, Rio de Janeiro, Brazil.

Yael Padan, The Bartlett School of Architecture, University College London, London, UK.

Sandra Guinand, EIREST, University of Paris 1 Panthéon-Sorbonne, Paris, France; Institute of Geography and Regional Research, Vienna University, Vienna, Austria.

Jean-François Staszak, Geography Department of the University of Geneva, Geneva, Switzerland.

Lu Yue, EIREST, University of Paris 1 Panthéon-Sorbonne, Paris, France.

Introduction

simulacra, architecture, tourism and the Uncanny

Nelson Graburn, Gravari-Barbas Maria and Staszak Jean-François

Introduction

This is the first time in History that the same products are consumed in stores that are all the same, in any large city in the world.
Those architectural copies reflect the questions of our time:
the uprooting of cultures, the virtualization of our lives, marketing applied to heritage …
Such constructions are much more than concrete blocks built just to impress.
They are concrete utopia brought to life. They are the expression of a dream … '
Umberto Eco

Simulacra, architecture and tourism: a system analysis

The topic of this collection of papers builds on the articulation between simulacra, architecture and tourism. It rests squarely on the notion of *simulation* and the more specialized word *simulacra*. Thus, it is concerned with various forms of likeness or similarity, but *not* identity. The case studies presented examine and analyze different kinds of architectural copies, with varying relations to originals, even if the originals are themselves copies of previous originals. In some cases, we know little or nothing of the first in the series. It may even happen that the original did not actually exist.

This topic is therefore highly compatible with, derivative or even part of the history of architecture. Serious works on the history of architecture, as a whole (e.g. Copplestone & Seton, 1963; Renault & Lazé, 2006) or volumes concerned with particular cultural regions, temporal periods or artistic styles, focus on both continuity and creativity. A focus on simulacra concentrates more on the micro-interplay between copies and changes, or more generally, familiarity and alterity.

We can see the direct parallels with tourist motivations. Tourists are also looking for a balance of novelty and similarity, of alterity and familiarity. Tourism, in the European world, started in the seventeenth century with the Grand Tour, in which the upper class (youth) of Northern Europe spent months or a year traveling and visiting more southerly regions and the Mediterranean. This was a qualified alterity: the visitors, with guides or tutors, were visiting related civilizations, but ones strongly connected to their classical Romans and Greek cultural ancestors, as rediscovered during the Renaissance[1] – which was itself an almost global effort to reconnect with historical and archaeological alterity and hence to build or consolidate identities. Thus the tourists were looking for experiences and landscapes that were different from home, yet familiar through the tourist imaginary built upon their classical education. Even within this purview they might find simulacra, in the many Roman copies of Greek originals, not only in architecture, but in culture and literature.

Since then there has emerged a wide range of kinds of tourists (Cohen, 1979; Graburn, 2017; Smith, 1977), among whom the vast majority are only seeking selected and temporary elements of otherness. As Graburn (1983a, pp. 22–23) pointed in the Introduction to the *Annals of Tourism Research* special issue on Anthropology, if tourism is considered a kind of ritual inversion (cf. Leach, 1961) then most tourists remain within a basically similar life style, and rarely choose to 'invert' more than a few factors, e.g. from a strict to a loose schedule, from formal to informal kinds of dress, or from sexual restraint to promiscuity. Few change their basic identity or sexual orientation, gender, name, religion, or their orientation to home and alterity, with the exception of Cohen's 'existentials' who may become self-exiles or migrants (1979).

The point here is that the tourists' conscious focus might be on obvious novelty or distinctions – of climate, food, leisure style, most of their orientations, like architectural simulations, remain within the realm of the familiar. Tourist photography, for instance, is a combination of recording the iconic distinctive features[2] of the environment or destination, as well 'the familiar out there' in the family or group photo, *kinen shashin*[3] and of course, 'selfies'.

Architecture: degrees of familiarity and strangeness

The cases described and analysed in this volume represent a whole range of 'copies,' that is the relationship between the buildings observed and some real or mythical original. Just as the meaning of simulacra has been subject to a wide range of interpretations in the literature, even Baudrillard (1981) considers four major types of relations between truth and hyperreality: (1) Basic reflections of reality, counterfeits, obvious fakes that draw attention away from reality (2) Perversions of reality, where there is multiple production of false images, differentiation is between signs, not signs and reality (3) Pretenses of reality, where there is no known original, and there we stop expecting to differentiate reality from fiction (4) Simulacra which bears no relation to reality – it is an invention *sui generis*; such 'copies' pretend to 'be reality' to build a false world view e.g. we know that Disneyland is not a 'real place' but it fools us into thinking that the rest of America is 'real.' So hyperreality is more real than real, in that it contains its own origin myth which does not/cannot be checked 'against reality.' Though Baudrillard focuses on Hollywood and American productions, we could read the same lessons from the Old World plethora of Santa Clauses or Crucifixes which embody the mythology that there was an original which is impossible to check. Applied to architectural situations, these layers or alternate ways of copying stretch our imagination on the variety of simulations and the nature of their alterities.

Baudrillard's and Eco's (1986) critiques of Disney theme parks and of the USA as the land of simulacra express a very European point of view, which might be suspected of showing some elitist and Americanophobic bias. On the one hand and as we just mentioned, simulacra are the monopoly neither of the USA nor of postmodernity. On the other hand, they are important landmarks, visited by billions of people and much significant in popular culture (Gottdiener, 2001; Lukas, 2013, 2016). Visitors of theme parks and themed shopping malls genuinely enjoy these places as such. More attention (and respect?) should be paid to the visitors' motivations, pleasure and performance. Tourism studies have argued that the tourists should stop being seen as the 'idiot du voyage' (Urbain, 1991): accordingly, places that tourists love to visit should be taken seriously and not be reduced to and discredited because their alleged fakery.

The papers in this collection present examples of different kinds of 'copies' whereby a building, usually in or even central to a tourist destination, is knowingly some kind of copy of another building or architectural design usually elsewhere. The range of relationships of these buildings to their 'originals' far outspans the imagination and consideration of Baudrillard and others. Most of the planners of these destinations or the creators of these iconic buildings choose to construct them because the 'original' building or design is well known, and a tourist attraction in its right and presumably will lend 'fame,' an aura (Benjamin, 1936) and drawing power to the new destination. However, there are variations within this simple plan and some cases go well beyond this model.

The complexity of 'buildings as copies' becomes apparent where we begin to examine the nature of each of the components in the above model. The building or set of buildings under consideration are said to be copies of another building (or design). But the different dimensions of 'copies' should be analyzed in relation with the scope or the goal of the produced counterfeits, reinterpretations, pretenses of reality or pure creations (simulacra).

One simple dimension is *scale* – is the 'copy' under consideration the same size as the original, a miniature or a gigantic reproduction? Scale plays a major role indeed and the uncountable number of Eiffel towers around the world, from key holders to 'real' tourist attractions, may illustrate the different parallel lives of a major tourist icon.

Another dimension is the *nature of the copy*: an 'exact' replica, a copy that 'looks like' the original but differs on close inspection, a copy that is 'in the style or tradition of' the original, trending into a stereotype or caricature, often a commoditized model of some famous original. And here we have to ask, *who* would know or care about how exact or similar the copy is – the creators, the destination planners, the tourists from elsewhere or from the region of the original, or the locals in the destination?

Our task is extended by some of the examples in this collection and other possibilities. When a copy-building, called Duplitecture in one of the papers, actually *does not have an existing original*. It might be copied after a photograph or a painting of a building, a detailed description of it, a set of drawing or designs, a memory, a dream, a (historical) myth, a story or even just a name! And again we must ask, which of the many stakeholders know or think or believe in the similarity – and what do they think of it? The 'Haussmannian' buildings in Tianducheng (China) are not 'copies' of any existing Haussmannian building in Paris but their quintessential reinterpretations. The fact they are *not* exact copies does not prevent the visitors from having 'real' impressions of being in a Parisian-style setting.

Again, we may focus on the *nature of the original*. Is it a unique original building, at least at the time it was copied, or it is a known kind of original, such as an English medieval castle or a triumphal arch? Even where there is a known unique original building, there are debates about *what should be copied*; if a building changes or evolves over time, as most do, what is the 'real' original to be copied? In Japan there has been a debate about the preservation or copying of traditional *minka*, farm houses, whether the best preserved example or copy should resemble the pure original design or the latest version with all the excrescences such as a car garage, TV antennae, electrification or so on (Ehrentraut, 1989, 1993).

And in our cases and others, the original may have been *unique but may no longer exist*, having been destroyed by nature (earthquakes, landslides, the sea), by enemy action or by modernization schemes. The nature and ability to copy depends on how long ago the building disappeared, was it copied or modeled, are there plans, or paintings or photographs or good literary descriptions, or perhaps memories? Most of these latter questions are unanswerable only in the scope of experts and may be full of guesses.

And of course, a simulacrum does *not* need to refer to an original. The 'medieval' castle of Guédelon, in Burgundy, build with 'authentic' material according to the medieval ways of building, in a place in which a medieval castle could have been eventually built, does not refer to any precise castle. It summarizes the archetypal features of a mediaeval castle and succeeds into conveying a message that a ruined 'authentic' castle could not.

The role of tourism in the production of simulacra

It appears that copies, reinterpretations and simulacra are the essence of architecture. Architecture historians showed that the buildings of the antiquity, medieval or classic times have been, and still are, an endless inspiration for architects. What interests us here is however the role tourism played in this reinvention, as a modern phenomenon which interferes with architecture. From its beginnings, in the industrial revolution, an era that heralded the rapid urbanization of Western Europe, the phenomenon of mass tourism inspired built environments that have a constitutive, and sometimes problematic, relationship with the architectural references from which the draw their inspiration. On the one hand, such environments reinterpret architectural and urban archetypes such as the ancient palace, the Renaissance villa, or the Mediterranean village. On the other hand, they spatialize perceptions of utopia: among them, pristine environments, Shangri-La, El Dorado, Eden, and Paradise. In most cases these two situations occur simultaneously, creating idealized places inspired by dreamed or utopian ideas.

The analysis of Las Vegas hotels (Gravari-Barbas, 2001) offers an almost complete range of the source of inspirations – not only in

> Las Vegas, but as more general references of tourism settings. We found the most emblematic tourist cities (Paris (Hotel Paris Las Vegas), Venice (Hotel The Venetian), New York (Hotel New York, New York), Monte Carlo (hotel Monte Carlo); historical and geographical periods such as antique Rome (hotel Caesar's) or ancient Egypt (Hotel Luxor); 'exotic' worlds such as the Caribbean (hotel Treasure Island) or fairy worlds (Hotel Excalibur).

Tourists are not only the 'consumers' of these idealized worlds; they also co-produce and they constantly re-interpret them through their imaginaries and their practices. Non-Western practices of tourism are similarly inspired to build their simulacra based on their imaginaries of both the 'traditional Western world' (e.g. Shenzen, Windows on the World) and their virtual worlds (e.g. Hindu Temple theme parks). If these tourism worlds have been inspired by actually existing places as well as imagined worlds, then they have also inspired, in their turn, the places in which we live, work, learn, shop, study or practice our leisure activities.

Copies, pretenses of realities and simulacra

We can now see that our selection of architectural cases studies makes Baudrillard (1981) and Deleuze's (1968) extrapolation of frames and simulation into simulacra appear rather simplistic. The main problems with their works, ironically, is the absence of consideration of the range and contexts of human motivations or purpose. Let us briefly examine our main cases along with a few other examples before a concluding discussion. We will endeavor to move from the simpler cases of replication through the various types to the most abstruse or complex, perhaps going beyond the archetypal meaning of 'simulacra.'

Bauer and Canestrini plunge headlong into the well-worn debates (MacCannell, 1976; Urry, 1990; Wang, 1999) about tourists' search for authenticity vs. mere amusement or distraction (Cohen, 1979). They show that replicas of famous buildings, which they call duplitecture, are common at commercial destinations where the tourists are not searching for authenticity but for entertainment. They claim that the tourists enjoy the 'fakelore,' fully understanding on their collective enjoyment (Feifer, 1985), that these are not originals, but drawing attention to and thereby elevating the status of the originals – 'The clone can be seen as an appetizer for the UNESCO world heritage site … ' This is a partial contradiction to Benjamin's assertion that modern mechanical reproduction diminishes the *aura* – the emotional/historical impact – of the original. But perhaps the plainly commercial copies are not quite the 'mass mechanical reproductions' of Benjamin's thesis.

One focus of their paper is the Chinese replication of the UNESCO-recognized Austrian village of Hallstatt, initially planned for local use as offices and apartments in Guangzhou, now becoming a tourism attraction. The power and meaning of this copy were totally different for the Chinese seeing the original (as tourists) because for them the copy is the original. And the Austrians seeing the copy, which was done without notice or permission, produced a momentary uncanniness – they couldn't believe their eyes – followed by pride and then by opportunism as a chance to attract tourists to the 'real' place. Bauer and Canestrini point out that most famous historical and classical buildings (and art works) are to a great degree and purposively, made as copies, e.g. l'Odeon in Paris, the Pantheon in Rome, the Great Pyramid of Cheops. Thus replication is the norm, not the exception.

Loureiro and Bartholo make roughly the same point, using a different lexicon and basis for analysis. They start by affirming that, following Harries (1997), architecture is a representational art, where each building represents ('copies') previous ones in some ways. They too refer to cases of Chinese replication of European buildings or townscapes, calling them not duplitecture but simulacrascapes. They try to show that Chinese conceptions of replication are not as simple as European notions of copying, presenting an array of kinds of copies of decreasing exactness, rather like the discussion above. Unlike Bauer and Canestrini who accept duplitecture as an acceptable norm for commercial purposes and tourist destinations, Loureiro and Bartholo raise the common moral question about authenticity (cf. MacCannell, 1976) and, following Buber, distinguish between the mere body (appearance) of the building, which may be a fake, and its soul (inner meaning). Not only does this apply to kinds of copies but also to the tourist experience whether the visitor takes the time an effort to engage with the 'thou' rather than the reflexive 'I'. But they too make the same point that most famous historic European buildings are 'representations' of earlier buildings.

In an useful consideration, Loureiro and Bartholo pursue architecture as representation, suggesting that any one building represents a previous one in an attempt to represent 'an image of an ideal' behind that original, e.g. the Pantheon in Paris as a representation of the 'original' in Rome and in turn as a classical Roman memorial temple, or the Chinese replica of Hallstatt as a model European [Austrian] village. This suggests that in all cases of duplitecture or *copie conforme* ['true copies'], a mental construct may well lie behind any 'original' recalling an aesthetic style, a historical period, a cultural or religious purpose or a geographically-based stereotype. They illustrate this with two contrasting examples: Chinese and other copies of Venice which 'do not actually celebrate the original, but banalize it,' for Chinese who do not know or care about its authenticity, with the relationship of 'I' not 'Thou,' as opposed to the transformation of Rio de Janeiro in the century after the fall of Napoleon into a 'Tropical Paris' as a simulation of not only Paris but of a true 'European capital city.'

In her discussion of the creation of the Ratatouille attraction of Paris Disneyland, Gravari-Barbas goes straight to the same point. The creators of Disneyland never intended to represent Paris as a whole or in reality, but to present the visitor with a carefully selected array of characteristic but often subtle features of urban Paris by 'recycling geographical imaginaries' such that the visitor feels they are in Paris, even though they may not know why they feel that way. Designers avoided obvious iconic buildings, unlike the many destinations which include representations of the Eiffel Tower. Working from photographs, they picked out common 'street life' features which the potential visitors would have seen in the myriad media representations of Paris experienced by inhabitants of the modern world.

In this context, Paris-Las Vegas, with its pastiche of off-scale models of the Eiffel Tower, the Opera, Moulin Rouge, Arc de Triomphe, the Louvre etc. is the opposite to the streetscapes of Ratatouille which could be anywhere in the stereotype of Haussmannesque Paris. She proposes that as this is not a copy of a particular place in Paris, it is a simulacrum, a copy without an original. But, she concludes than in fact the circle is completed, for the street features of Ratatouille are copied from originals which are in the tourist imaginaries, which are representations of images in Paris from a billion screen views, which are copies …. .

Padan's analysis of representations of pre-Roman conquest (before 70 CE) Jerusalem highlights the problem of scale as well as the temporal loss of knowledge about the 'original,' suggested another route to simulacra, in the simple sense of a copy without an original. Padan notes that the original 1960s touristic model of 'old Jerusalem' featured by a hotel there, changed its meaning when it was moved to the Israel Museum, changing its meaning from a tourist-historic attraction to a national religious object. This model inspired others: one Yeshivah (Orthodox Jewish seminary) in the Old City commissioned a larger 1:60 scale model of the Second Temple on the Mount (Herod's Temple), destroyed 1900 years ago, and placed it on the roof so it overlooks the Muslim occupied Mount, suggesting the long-promised rebuilding of a Third Temple on the Mount. The creator said he was inspired by a dream, for there are no illustrations or models from the Second Temple, only myths and archaeological ruins.

Conversely the Orlando, Florida Holyland Experience built a half size model of Herod's Temple (the height of a 6-storey building!) in which visitors could engage in 'biblical experiences' and watch videos in the auditorium both for Christians to renew their Faith and for Jews to be converted to Christianity. Even larger is the oversized 74,000 m-2 model of Solomon's Temple (the First Temple), said to have lasted approx. 1,000–600 BCE., as a church in Sao Paulo, Brazil. This 10,000 seat building is the headquarters church of a Pentecostal sect with 1.8 million members. Built with materials from Israel, to give the visitors/worshippers an authentic feeling of holiness, this Church may or may not resemble Solomon's temple of which there are no records and few descriptions (and controversy whether it in fact existed). While the Jerusalem model allows visual access to the ancient city, the two larger replica temples allow visitors the special feelings of being able to circulate within 'the temple.' But the question of simulacra is enhanced by the poor or absent knowledge of the ancient temples themselves and the fact that the replicas may also serve as optimistic 'copies of' the envisioned future Third Temple – a simulacrum of an original that has never existed but will in the future!

Yu, Gravari-Barbas and Guinand bring us a somewhat more complex case of a building as simulacrum. In this case, the recently rebuilt (2014) Minyuan Stadium in Tianjin, China, has seen many transformations, since its original as a sports stadium, built in 1926, with a European residential concession in the then garden city suburb. Nearly destroyed in the war (1943), later rebuilt smaller with clay replacing the grass surface in 1954; after the 1979 earthquake it was again rebuilt with bigger stands for soccer. It was closed in 2012 and rebuilt as part of a large cultural, leisure center in 2014. None of these changes attempted to replicate the original, but all rebuilt for the needs and purposes of the day. After the 2005 founding of the Tianjin Historical Restoration & Development company, the stadium has been developed and reintegrated into the high end plan for attracting the rich and the foreign to this historically significant area, with 'cafés, wine and cigars bars, fusion food, as well as art galleries and a museum of traditional Chinese art. The place also hosts different cultural activities (exhibitions, concerts, etc.)'. The Minyuan stadium does not pretend to be a copy of any (past) real building, but it is 'trans-temporal simulacrum' which represents a prestigious historic period of European influence, engendered as much by its name rather than its form. As a commercial and cultural success (30–60,000 visitors a day) – and a visitor center – it has become a destination for visitors who have little or no idea about the original stadium, save for an aura of important sports events and a cosmopolitan history as a node on the foreign quarters.

Gordon's research on the Musée de la Grande Guerre du Pays de Meaux [Museum of the Great War, Pays de Meaux region] just north of Paris, brings up two pertinent questions. In what ways are museums inherently simulacra, and could its displays really be true replicas of a great war? MacCannell (1976) succinctly described museum exhibitions of two types: classes of objects, e.g. sets of arrowheads or collections of clothing, or dioramas, attempting to display people or objects in a 'natural' setting. Obviously only that latter is a concern for our consideration of copies and simulation.

Gordon's analysis is, like others', concerned with authenticity of the simulation, but he judges this case more strictly than our other authours. He points out the near impossibility of recreating the full sensory experience of past events, noting the lack of real 'war sounds,' and no attempt at reproducing the appalling smells (of cordite, rotting foods, medical salves etc.)[4] of the trench living experience. Gordon also makes the point that the behavior of visitors themselves in the museum and its grounds, as well as the presence of the postwar American war memorial, prevent the displays from closely simulating the 'original' trench warfare experience. Returning to Baudrillard's indictments, 'The world of simulacra for Baudrillard is precisely a postmodern world of signs without depth, origins, or referent. (Best & Kellner, n.d.)' he assures us that the Musée de la Grand Guerre is neither postmodern nor is it a simulacrum.

Buchrieser's comparison of the extraordinary histories of Charles Mackintosh's architectural buildings and ideas in Glasgow and Gaudi's works in Barcelona stretches our consideration of simulacra and facsimiles beyond prior imaginations. Though most of our case studies focus on duplitecture in (potential) tourist destinations, based on famous originals elsewhere, Buchrieser's cases focus mostly on the reproduction or reinterpretation of architectural works in their original places, attempting to enhance local distinctiveness by enhancing what is already present.

Gaudi's case is the simpler, but is unusual that many of his works, especially the Sagrada Familia cathedral, were not fully built, or even designed in Gaudi's lifetime. Thus, though in part they are posthumous interpretations (sometimes altered) of designs left by Gaudi, much of the later work, financed almost entirely by (and built for) tourists, are simulacra to the extent that they are copies of non-existent originals, dreamed up more freely by later architects.[5]

Mackintosh's Glasgow architectural heritage is almost entirely posthumous and stretches architectural imagination beyond rationality and perhaps legality. His 'House for an Art Lover', eventually built in 1996 was designed in 1901 but never built. When the lost plans came to light, the executive architect Roxburgh, reinterpreted the domestic house as a visitor center adapted for commercial priorities and events. Though Buchrieser attests that it is a simulacrum, not really having original, the vast majority of hordes of visitors believe it really is a Mackintosh building, bringing fame and fortune to the park and to Glasgow (and to Macintosh). In the case of the four tea rooms designed by Mackintosh, only the Willow Tea Rooms survived.[6] These have been redeveloped, new rooms added with the same themes, other tea rooms opened with some original features and furniture. The new owner patented the name and built complete simulacra on other streets, and developed new named rooms following in part Mackintosh designs. Mackintosh's designs (mainly tea rooms) have become a brand[7] which attracts visitors who don't know the difference, and display the occasional real Mackintosh items. The Willow Tea Rooms have been bought by a trust, to be donated to the City of Glasgow, self-financed by the tourist crowds,[8] like the Sagrada Familia.

Discussion

Tourists, like human beings almost everywhere, are motivated by both novelty and familiarity. They need novelty (alterity) to break the mundane boredom of unchanging lives (similarity). And they need a structure of familiarity is order to be able to judge, and appreciate the new.[9] As we have mentioned the balance between the familiar and the novel varies immensely between types of tourists, their home cultures, their class positions, their life stages and so on. The history of architecture reflects the same human emotions. The vast majority of buildings are minor modifications of familiar local styles which, over time show evolution into new forms and types. These changes are aided by technological breakthroughs as well as by travel to unfamiliar places. Even technological breakthroughs may be resisted by buildings retaining familiar aesthetic features from former material traditions, skeuomorphs, as far back a Greek stone temples and in today's hi-tech creations which may retain elements of roof slopes, columns, etc. which are completely unnecessary.

While people in their home environment appreciate familiarity and variety, they are often upset with complete breaks with tradition, styles that are 'out of place' or which are 'out of time' anachronisms. Most tourists expect more novelty when they travel, though, as MacCannell notes, for most the novelties are actually familiar as icons or brands of the known tourist destination they are visiting. Again a balance of familiarity and novelty. Architectural simulations, as we have seen, may be known in advance, such as copies of Venice or the Eiffel Tower, but for those familiar with the originals, the degree of accuracy is emotionally significant. Following the idea of the Uncanny Valley (Mori, 2012) we know that exact replicas and very poor copies are interesting[10] but that almost-exact copies cause the visitor to do a 'double take,' to have an uncanny troubling feeling, perhaps an aversion at first. This troubling but eye-opening combination or alterity and familiarity is what makes tourism attractive and what encourages planners and designers to create duplitecture in tourist destinations.

There is no pristine or 'authentic' place/people that tourists could visit/encounter, the tourists' presence, gaze and supposed expectations necessarily inducing some kind of staging. Hence, tourists do not enjoy authenticity but rather a 'staged authenticity' (Mac-Cannell, 2013) that most of the time they are well aware of and happy with. But what about those who enjoy simulacra, and appreciate the place they visit and the people they encounter not in spite of their fakery but because of it? Simulacra are 'authentic fakery' (AlSayyad, 2001). Their visitors perfectly fit the definition of the post-tourist, a « consumer who embraces openly, but with some irony, the increasingly inauthentic, commercialized and simulated experiences offered by the tourism industry » (Smith, Macleod, & Robertson, 2010, p. 130). For the post-tourist, the authenticity of the place is not an issue anymore, but the authenticity of the experience still is: it becomes the product (Pine & Gilmore, 1999; Tyrell & Mai, 2001).

Notes

1. This relates closely to the uncanny, the *unheimlich*, though vaguely known to be connected, these cultural ancestors had been hidden over time, and were revealed as both different and familiar, *étrangement troublant* by the literary and archaeological researchers of the Renaissance.
2. According to MacCannell (2013) modern tourism consists of itineraries linking societally known or approved sites which are the distinctive features of other places; they are named and are the 'familiar within the unfamiliar', the ones that most of the members of the traveler's home group would recognize.
3. The very apt Japanese phrase meaning roughly the 'memorial photo' or the photo of record, necessary in the 'traditional' Japanese tourism system (Graburn, 1983b) for demonstrating to those left at home, who often provided money, clothing, camera equipment to the travelers, that the travelers did indeed visit the expected places.
4. The only comparable site I (Graburn) know, which tries to represent smells accurately is the Jorvik Viking Centre in York. UK. This underground archaeological site is experienced from a slow 'boat ride' through the reconstructed Viking town of 975 CE, with the appropriate

smells, sounds – including hearing Old Norse – heat, cold and dampness, and period manne-quins with faces reconstructed after Viking skulls! Some have criticized this popular attraction as being too Disneyesque.
5. Buchrieser also mentions the case of a chapel about to be built in Chile more than 100 years after Gaudi completed the designs, which were lost for over seventy years.
6. Most were destroyed by rebuilding but features of some interiors were preserved in the Willow Tea Rooms and a museum.
7. Like Gaudi's chapel to the built in Chile, a Japanese company wanted to recreate the brand overseas but the project never materialized.
8. 150,000 p.a. for the Tea Rooms and 50,000 for the Visitor Centre (the ex-House for an Art Lover).
9. As in the Greek phrase "'Δός μοι πᾷ στῶ καὶ τὰν γᾶν κινήσω'" (Give me a firm spot to stand and I will move the world.(Archimedes)
10. Like a Teddy Bear and a real bear, or a stuffed real bear. However the appearance of a corpse or a life-like robot causes a momentary jarring frisson until the situation is fully comprehended.

Disclosure statement

No potential conflict of interest was reported by the authors.

References

AlSayyad, N. (Ed.). (2001). *Consuming tradition/manufacturing heritage: Global norms and urban forms in an age of tourism*. New York: Routledge.

Baudrillard, J. (1981). *Simulacres and simulation*. Paris: Galilée.

Benjamin, W. (1936). Ĺœuvre d´art à ĺépoque de sa reproduction méchanisée. [The work of art in the age of mechanical reproduction.]. *Zeitschrift für Sozialforschung, 5*, 40–68.

Best, S., & Kellner, D. (n.d.). Debord and the postmodern turn: New stages of the spectacle. *Illuminations*. Retrieved from http://www.uta.edu/huma/illuminations/kell17.htm

Cohen, E. (1979). A phenomenology of tourist experiences. *Sociology, 13*, 179–201.

Copplestone, T., & Seton, L. (1963). *World architecture: An illustrated history*. London: Hamblyn.

Deleuze, G. (1968). *Difference and repetition*. (Paul Patton, Trans.). New York: Columbia University Press.

Eco, U. (1986). *Travels in hyper-reality*. London: Picador.

Ehrentraut, A. (1993). Heritage authenticity and domestic tourism in Japan. *Annals of Tourism Research, 20*(2), 262–278.

Ehrentraut, A. W. (1989). The visual definition of heritage: The restoration of domestic rural architecture in Japan. *Visual Anthropology, 2*, 135–161.

Feifer, M. (1985). *Going places*. London: Macmillan.

Gottdiener, M. (2001). *The theming of America: American dreams, media fantasies, and themed environments* (2nd ed). Boulder, CO: Westview.

Graburn, N. (1983a). The anthropology of tourism. In: Nelson Graburn (ed.) The anthropology of tourism. Special Issue of *Annals of Tourism Research* 10: (1): 9–33.

Graburn, N. (1983b). *To pray, pay and play: The cultural structure of Japanese domestic tourism*. Aix-en-Provence: Centre es Hautes Etudes Touristiques.

Graburn, N. (2017). "The Tourist" Chapter 7. In Noel B. Salazar (ed.) In *Key figures of human mobility*. Special issue of *Social Anthropology/Anthropologie Sociale*) 25 (1): 83–96. doi:10.1111/1469-8676.12394.

Gravari-Barbas, M. (2001). La leçon de Las Vegas, le tourisme dans la ville festive. *Géocarrefour*, Revue de Géographie de Lyon, Vol. 76, No 2, Le tourisme et la ville, Lyon pp. 169–165.

Harries, K. (1997). *The ethical function of architecture*. Cambridge, MA: MIT Press.

Leach, E. R. (1961). *Rethinking anthropology*. London: Athlone Press.

Lukas, S. A. (Ed.). (2013). *The immersive worlds handbook: Designing theme parks and consumer spaces*. New York: Focal.

Lukas, S. A. (Ed.). (2016). *A reader in themed and immersive spaces*. Pittsburgh, PA: Carnegie Mellon University/ETC Press.

MacCannell, D. (1976). *The tourist. A new theory of the leisure class*. New York: Schocken Paperbacks.

MacCannell, D. (2013). *The tourist: A new theory of the leisure class*. Berkeley: University of California Press.

Mori, M. (2012). The Uncanny Valley [From the field]. *IEEE Robotics & Automation Magazine, 19*(2), 98–100. [Translated by MacDorman, K. F.; Kageki, Norri.].

Pine, J., & Gilmore, J. (1999). *The experience economy*. Boston: Harvard Business School Press.

Renault, C., & Lazé, C. (2006). *Les styles de l'architecture et du mobilier*. Paris: Gisserot.

Smith, V. (1977). *Hosts and guests*. Philadelphia: Univ. of Pennsylvania Press.

Smith, M., Macleod, N., & Robertson, M. H. (2010). *Key concepts in tourist studies*. London: SAGE.

Tyrell, B., & Mai, R. (2001). *Leisure 2010. Experience tomorrow*. Henley: Jones Lang LaSalle.

Urbain, J.-D. (1991). *L'idiot du voyage. Histoires de touristes*. Paris: Plon.

Urry, J. M. (1990). *The tourist gaze: Leisure and travel in contemporary societies*. London: Sage.

Wang, N. (1999). Rethinking authenticity in tourism experience. *Annals of Tourism Research, 26*(2), 349–370.

Copysites: tourist attractions in the age of their architectural reproducibility

Bauer Bernhard and Canestrini Duccio

ABSTRACT
In this article we focus on those tangible assets that have been copied and imitated for reasons that are linked to tourism. What we call copysites are the replicas of places, buildings and sites that attract visitors interested in cultural heritage (tangible and intangible) and leisure activities, such as, entertainment, shopping, gastronomy etc. We analyse characteristic cases and acknowledge that the creation of copysites has different backgrounds: commercial interests, artistic and aesthetic motives, entertainment reasons, the joy to reproduce forms of success, preservation of the original sites, among others. We focus on who is content with visiting copies of monuments, sculptures, cities or 'fakelore' performances. On the basis of our examples we explain how far the principle of visiting replicated sites can be a success formula and why it seems so important for many tourists to see, check-in and tick-off activities and destinations, even if they are 'almost authentic'.

1. Introduction

Humanity has never travelled so much as in recent years. In 2030 UNWTO predicts international tourist arrivals to reach 1.8 billion thanks to the rise of emerging economies (2012). Every summer we are expected to go on holiday, take paid vacations, leave home and play tourist. As we need tangible evidence of our tourism activity, it is considered appropriate to bring home souvenirs as trophies of our travels (Canestrini, 2001, 2004). In David Lodge's novel *Paradise News* (1991) the tourism anthropologist Roger Sheldrake, who never goes on holiday, is writing his first book about 'tourism and the myth of paradise'. His theoretical approach is that 'people are not really enjoying themselves when they go on holiday, but engaging in a superstitious ritual' (p. 62). In this article we occasionally refer to Sheldrake's theory on the basis of copysites.[1]

We call copysites replicas or imitations of certain monuments or groups of buildings of outstanding universal value that have received global fame through the tourism and marketing industry. Too often such copysites are pejoratively stigmatised as fake buildings and downgraded to be visited by thoughtless tourists who are sight-seeing at the 'wrong' spots. The present article studies various kinds of copysites as tourist attractions in the light of the following three hypotheses: (i) historical tourist spots are neither pure nor immutable; (ii) tourism is performance; and (iii) copysites are inherently a business driven idea. Society, travel habits and motivations as well as destination marketing have undergone significant change and development in the last decades. Thus, we deem it relevant to analyse the mentioned hypotheses, in part related to Cohen's (1988) assumptions, from a contemporary point of view informed by rather recently created attractions as case studies.

Concerning the first hypothesis, we analyse the fact that tourist 'originals' undergo constant change. The dynamic processes that are combined with the commodification of assets are further linked to adaptations for our modern consumption and digital communication society. It has become difficult for travellers to distinguish between an authentic site and a copysite, moreover, travellers have different needs and expectations of a certain destination, and so it is delicate to argue whether it is 'better' to visit one or the other.

The article is based on the assumption that tourism and its corresponding industries are performances (Canestrini, 2003; Edensor, 2001; MacCannell, 1976). People go on compulsory holidays, travellers are collecting destinations and 'ticking off' sights from their must-travel list and the behaviour as a tourist has become routine for those who can afford to travel. MacCannell observed that 'the term "tourist" is increasingly used as a derisive label for someone who seems content with his obviously inauthentic experiences' (1973, p. 592). In addition to this, we argue that tourists are not constantly hunting for the ultimate authentic real world, as other scholars have pointed out (Brown, 1996; Ritzer & Liska, 1997). They might rather be 'collectively gazing' as Urry emphasises (1990), or carry with them a certain inability to have authentic experiences (Cohen, 1988). There are many tourist types (Cohen, 1979) and various reasons why visitors are enjoying seemingly superficial emotions, 'fakelore' performances or obvious replicas. The chosen examples describe cases of different justifications for the motivations of visitors.

Regarding the contested, yet highly relevant concept of authenticity in tourism related research we adopt Wang's (1999, 2000) identification of the three dominant and different approaches to understanding authenticity, which are 'objective', 'constructed' and 'existential'. While the latter is 'activity-related', the others are 'object-related'. He observed that tourism is an 'industry of authenticity' (2000, p. 71) where the actively-related form of existential authenticity becomes a commodity. What Wang defined as 'toured objects' can be compared with the here used term of copysites which are 'totally inauthentic' but the 'existential version is a justifiable alternative source for authentic experiences in tourism' (1999, p. 365). With the presentation of several examples, this article argues about the justification for the construction of copysites as well as the justification of tourists visiting them.

In our opinion, copysites are commercially driven business activities. Moreover, they are plainly beneficial for the destinations where they were constructed and we intend to contribute to the de-stigmatising such places. We also deal with the controversial issue of commodification of culture in its positive and negative aspects (Bauer, 2014, 2016). Certainly, the de-contextualisation of tangible and intangible cultural heritage is rooted in terms of an anthropological critical approach, while from a practical point of view the advantages of 'duplitecture' are undeniable for destinations and its visitors.

We use terms such as 'tourism product' and 'commodity' when we write about cultural elements, which have been or are in process of being transformed, hence commodified, into consumable and saleable products (Gotham, 2007). In this context we apply Bourdieu's concept of symbolic goods – these '(…) are a two-faced reality, a commodity and a symbolic object. Their specifically cultural value and their commercial value remain relatively independent, although the economic sanction may come to reinforce their cultural consecration' (1993, p. 113). On the one hand, art is produced according to a logic, which is heteronomous with respect to the logic of economic profit. If produced for commercial success it is discordant with the dominant logic of arts. On the other hand, its production is autonomous with respect to the economic field and therefore created for enhancing symbolic capital or prestige. This is valued and its success is determined by the approval of other autonomous cultural producers (p. 39). Appadurai (1986) deals with the significance of such commodities in their socio-cultural contextualisation and in particular with the emergence of their significance for the relation among individuals and groups regarding consumption.

With reference to the social structure of tourism sites, MacCannell (1973) following Goffman (1959) distinguishes between front and back regions of certain destinations. The front region is defined as 'the meeting place of host and guest' and presumed a 'show' while the back region is a space where only locals have access to and thus defines an 'intimate' and 'real' part of social life at a destination. In light of Goffman's distinction we argue that copysites and their social spaces are primarily a front region of an alien destination.

2. Copysites and their architectural reproducibility[2]

When we speak about copysites and try to understand their meaning we might first need to recognise where they come from. In terms of monumental tourist attractions copysites immanently arise from original sites. Such sites of outstanding universal relevance (statuary works, buildings, edifices and architectonical structures) have a historical value and so they recall and represent historical processes. Throughout history original sites have often been subject to change in different manners including visible architectonical modifications (inside or outside), alterations to their initial purpose, adaptations, misunderstandings, political manipulations, modernisations (be it electricity or security measures, access for disabled persons, elevators, etc.), or simply through a process of decay due to missing commitment or financial funds. Therefore, original sites cannot be defined as undiluted or pure forms that have always remained in the same 'original' state. They are dynamic structures that are adapted to human longings and needs throughout history.

In relation to historical or modern original sites: we could allege that the Taj Mahal is a copy of an older mausoleum somewhere in India and the Burj Khalifa is a copy of the Empire State Building. Copies and imitations of monumental sites have always existed. Today's remnants of ancient Roman temples and theatres have been copied in early times both from Etruscan and Greek examples. New erections of architectonical buildings have been trying to imitate others. With slight or profound alterations this turned out to be the evolution of architecture and keeps evolving until today: there will always be a higher skyscraper, somewhere, which quotes a 'twin'.

Some copies have in the meantime become originals in their own right like Michelangelo's David in Florence. The biblical figure of David has been sculptured by many artists (Donatello 1440, Verrocchio 1475, Bernini 1623) but the one by Michelangelo Buonarroti, finished in 1504 is aesthetically said to be the most beautiful artwork and hence more famous than others (although it is criticised that his right hand is slightly larger and not perfectly proportional to the rest of the body). After having spent almost 400 years in front of the *Palazzo Vecchio*, David was moved to the *Galleria dell'Accademia* in 1872. Weather and animals contributed to the material degradation of the fragile white marble and conservationists wanted to have him protected with a roof above his head. Thanks to this action the *Galleria* has become the second most visited museum in Florence in the last decades. In 1910 a replica was erected at the exact former position in *Piazza della Signoria*. In 1911 another replica of David (in bronze) was put in *Piazzale Michelangelo*. Today, these replica statues are more commonly visited and photographed than the real David in the museum. They have become almost originals. In this case we actually have a rare example of a historical commodification of cultural heritage. Nobody would regard those copies as fake Davids.

Both concepts, the original and the replica, have been defined and discussed from different points of view across various academic disciplines. We could list numerous conceptual categories and definitions that have been published by scholars in fields such as philosophy (Baudrillard, 1983), semiotics (Eco, 1986), history of art (Schwartz, 1996), social sciences (Benjamin, 1936; Bourdieu, 1993), just to name a few. Each of these disciplines give a contribution to our understanding of what is an original, a copy, a fake, a mimicry, a simulacrum and duplitechture.

In addition to these points of view of academic disciplines, there are cultural differences across the world in the understanding of what is an original and what is a copy. For example, in her book *Original Copies*, Bosker (2013) discusses the proliferation of copysites in China and claims this to be related to the Chinese concept of replica, which is different from Western perspectives. Bosker argues that in China a well made replica is considered appropriate and trustworthy, as opposed to less valuable than the original. Moreover, according to Fong (1962), there are four different understandings of a replica: *mu* means 'to trace' and heads after an exact replica (also regarding the replication of ruins); *lin* is the term for a copy or a looser replica; *fang* means 'to imitate' and can be an adaption of an original to the context; *tsao* means 'to invent', the original serves as an inspiration to the final work. In China, copied objects are understood as originals if they are 'created to bring an old style and maintain the spirit into the new' (Wang & Rowlands, 2017, p. 264). In the European context, copies definitely have lost the aura of the uniqueness of an original piece of art (Benjamin, 1936).

When we speak about copysites we also need to take into account the legal aspect of copyrights. While there are no royalties to pay when the historic town of Hallstatt is copied in China or the Eiffel Tower is reproduced in Las Vegas, sites replicated as miniature souvenirs or depicted on postcards are subject to intellectual property rights. For example, paintings, photographs, books, movies and music are normally subject to royalties if they are reproduced and sold on the market. Wang and Rowlands (2017) state that the missing idea of the 'fake' in Chinese art and heritage during the imperial era has resulted in a contradiction in the contemporary discourse of intellectual property rights in the global and Chinese context. A copyright is the 'legally protected entitlement of individuals or groups to control and to profit from the circulation, duplication, and sale of their creative work' (Comaroff & Comaroff, 2009, p. 33). Wong (2013) as well as de Kloet and Chow (2017) did research on the concept of duplicating art work in Dafen village, China. The local painters regard their work rather as performing an act of adaptation ('fang') and inno-vation ('tsao') instead of 'copying' western Masterpieces of Van Gogh, Warhol, and others. Wang and Rowlands argue that in China 'practices have blurred the boundary between fake and authentic in the arts world' (2017, p. 265). The question of 'who owns native culture' is posed by Brown (1998, 2003) in two different ways. There are, on the one side, those who protect intellectual property with laws, rights, and decrees such as the World Intellectual Property Organization or UNESCO with its Convention for the Safe-guarding of Intangible Cultural Heritage, among many others. On the other side, however, are those who maintain that culture is 'inherently public, organic, unbounded, and there-fore cannot be reduced to private property, individual or collective' (Comaroff & Comaroff, 2009, p. 30). The copyrighting of culture is according to the Comaroffs a rather modern mechanism of ethno-commodification.

3. Justifications for copysites

Copysites are not just created for replicating or imitating an original site. Each copysite has its specific justification and is used in various ways, not merely for tourism. This is exem-plified in the following cases.

The common rationale for copysites, though, is making profitable business. It is an attempt to reproduce alien cultural heritage at another destination or in another country. Making copysites is a successful model in times where 'culture means big business' (Bauer, 2016). Often, copysites pop up at destinations that need to reinvent themselves in order to stay attractive in the competitive global tourism market. At such destinations, copysites take up the role of an *Ersatzkultur*. Sometimes, these are places which lack historical developed tangible and intangible assets of global success and are thus dependent on importing and re-creating attractions that have proven to be success-ful in their original settings. As an example, the iconic nature of the Eiffel Tower, whether in Paris, Las Vegas or Shenzhen, attracts visitors anywhere due to its recognisability and popularity. The same is valid for the intangible heritage of the *Münchner Oktoberfest* and its many copies around the world, such as 'Wiener Wiesn' in Vienna, 'Hofbrauhaus' in Las Vegas, 'Oktoberfest Namibia' in Windhoek. These examples suggest that once a cul-tural heritage asset has been commodified successfully in terms of business development, it is often subject to being re-produced somewhere else and in a different context.

According to Lanfant (1995), once a cultural element is transformed into a tourist product, its cultural value is also transformed into a commercial value, a process which stimulates the reinvention of the past (Hobasbawm & Ranger, 1983). Rather than being a reclamation of the past, many elements of heritage and tourism work as new forms of cultural production – a kind of value-added industry (Kirshenblatt-Gimblett, 1998). The cul-tural value is usually framed in everyday life as profound, transcendent, creative, intrinsic, while the economic or commercial value is framed as superficial, repetitive, instrumental, calculative: one is supposed to be good, the other is consequently bad (Smith, 1988). Copysites are those reproductions of cultural elements that already have been commo-dified containing the commercial value only.

There are various definitions and uses of the term commodification in the social sciences. For example, Gotham (2007, p. 10) proposes a definition which is suitable for this research, and which sees commodification as a transformation of local cultural elements into consumable and saleable products (commodities), which are traded and sold for profitable exchange. In this sense, we apply the capitalist approach which assumes that anything that can be priced (tangible or intangible) can be sold, purchased, and consumed. As such, culture can be understood as a commodity, too (Burns & Novelli, 2006).

In their book *Ethnicity Inc.* the Comaroff and Comaroff (2009, p. 28) stress that the constant 'shift in the production of value from the material to the immaterial' through the trading and sale of intellectual property, identity, experiences, and so-called modes of self-production also indicates the fact that commerce 'exceeds the sale of goods and services'. Moreover, it is not just culture (with its traditions and expressions) that is increasingly commodified but that its commodity 'is being rendered explicitly cultural' – so the production and the consumption are focused on the intangible product of the experience. This means that the 'difference between marketing and consuming, and between living and buying is becoming smaller and smaller' (Comaroff & Comaroff, 2009, p. 28). In a similar vein, Tunbridge and Ashworth (1996) have analysed that the past is used as a resource and is increasingly being reshaped into a heritage commodity that serves present-day demands.

The commodification of culture for tourism purposes often coincides with a social and cultural influence, which certainly has to be differentiated in types of tourism and range of impact (Greenwood, 1977, p. 1989). Scholars of tourism-related topics have frequently 'begun their studies with a notion of tourism as something that is inherently "bad," due to the cultural degradation it is claimed to cause' (Shepherd, 2002, p. 183). Other exasperating consequences are false interpretations or low respect for local cultural values by visitors, transformation of local environments, etc. which are in conflict with the values and lifestyles of the local population.

Tourists themselves cannot be made responsible for displeasing impacts on the environment or congested city centres peppered with souvenir shops generating annoyance to the locals. Tourists follow their instinct of consuming related services and experiencing something new – and the local businesses follow the tourist demand. Mass tourist flows need to be channelled, managed and organised with the purpose of keeping locals, tourists, and businesses catering to the visitors satisfied.

Some copysites seem to fulfil beneficial preconditions because they are planned for being visited by high numbers of tourists. The sites can be described as comfortable places: all necessary direct tourist services such as restaurants, toilets, souvenir shops, site information, entertainment facilities, etc. are easily accessible. Potential disputes with the local population are rare since the chances for immediate contact are rather low. The sites tend to unload and relieve the congested original settings and generally appear as safe environments. Moreover, through the commercial character they attract investment within the value-chain, create jobs and awareness of the place through enhanced site promotion. The user-friendliness of copysites applies to intangible heritage assets as well. Cultural performances and shows that are fee-based reproductions of spectacles usually take place in neat and safe environments during theme-based events or in other business driven celebratory occasions.

For example, our fictitious, yet credible, protagonist Roger Sheldrake is alarmed about the carrying-capacity at tourist destinations. Original sites, where mass tourist flows are poorly organised, are often confronted with such issues: 'In 1987 they had to close

Venice one day because it was full. In 1963 forty-four people went down the Colorado river on a raft, now there are a thousand trips a day' (Lodge, 1991, p. 63). Historical cities like Florence and Barcelona have become victims of their own success, such that it is even suggested to put replicas of the cathedrals like *Santa Maria del Fiore* or *Sagrada Família* next to the airports (Canestrini, 2015, 2016). We can observe the issue of carrying-capacity as a worst-case scenario in the Venetian lagoon. The city authorities of Venice are hardly capable of keeping the masses off the islands or on the designated tourist paths – not even when the city is flooded and visitors are supposed to walk on improvised runways. Recently, Venice has been called the 'Disneyland on the sea' (Horowitz, 2017) where visitors need to put on their 'pollution masks' (Friedrich, 2017) due to the harmful toxic air pumped out by the world's largest cruise liners – though its mayor condemned this comparison and imputation. But in reality, Venice would need more of such negative press coverage so as to reduce the masses.

Venice's sister city in Las Vegas does not contribute to lower the visitor numbers in Italy. The US copysite offers its gamblers blue sky and carnival for 365 days a year, never-ending shopping facilities in imitations of Doge-style palazzi, singing *Gondoliere* on crystal clear waterways and the finest restaurants – flooding excluded. The replica gives the imagination of the perfect city and even fosters the will to travel to real Venice – but the original is quite different. This effect already happened to Eco (1986) after having visited Disneyland. He had the feeling that the imitations do not merely reproduce reality, but try improving on it.

Venice, perhaps the most copied place in the world, has become a brand and a commercial trend not just since the Venetian Resort Hotel in Las Vegas opened in 1999. In the United Arab Emirates soon the project 'Floating Venice' will be realised. In 2020 a hotel complex with 414 luxury suites will be finished 4 km off the coast of Dubai. The resort is supposed to spread the flair of Venice on floating platforms with rooms above and below sea level. The project does not aim at replicating Venice in detail but only takes its concept as a floating city (MacEwan, 2017). The same happens at the 'Louvre Abu Dhabi', a museum city on the Arabian gulf, which is not intended as a copy of the building complex of the Louvre of Paris. Louvre Abu Dhabi simply replicates the concept of the museum as a place where visitors can see and experience art galleries with exhibitions ranging from prehistoric artefacts to contemporary artwork. The term Louvre has become such a global synonym for excellence, preservation and exhibition of art that it is commodified as a brand.

The following case of a real-estate development that turned out to be an accidental replica represents a reverse process in which a UNESCO world heritage site ultimately became famous through its clone: Austria's town Hallstatt, tucked away in the Salzkammergut mountains on Lake Hallstatt with about 800 inhabitants. The almost exact copy of the town (church, mountains and lake included) was constructed in Luoyangzhen, province of Guangdong by the mining company China Minmetals as a real-estate investment for private apartments and office space. There was hardly any intention of creating an attraction for visitors. In 2011, the mayor of Hallstatt coincidentally learned about the Chinese copy when it was almost finished. While scepticism ruled at the beginning, he was quick to realise that this replication would have a positive effect on tourism for his own town. The opening ceremony of the complex took place a year later, during which the mayor of Hallstatt signed an agreement of cultural exchange and a traditionally dressed Alpine brass band accompanied the Chinese investors walking through the newly paved main square decorated with both typical Austrian flowers and untypical palm trees.

Retrospectively, the Chinese copysite can be seen as an 'appetizer' for the UNESCO world heritage site in Austria, and indeed, since 2012 the numbers of visitors have been rising continuously in Hallstatt. Annually there are up to 700,000 tourists visiting the town – this means an average of 1800 tourists a day hopping on and off the buses, arriving mainly from China, Japan, Korea and Thailand[3]. Due to increased overcrowding, Hallstatt has recently been thinking about a policy of limiting the daily entrances and has already implemented a 'no drone zone' (Müller, 2018). Locals have lamented about the increased air traffic and danger of drones taking pictures from above or flying pass their picturesque bathroom, kitchen and bedroom windows (Lanz, 2017) The information signs, showing a crossed-out drone, further urge the visitors to show respect to the people living in Hallstatt, keep off private property and use waste bins properly. The initiative was launched by the association of citizens for Hallstatt ('Bürgerliste Hallstatt') which turned into a local political party getting 28% of the votes in the local council elections in 2015 at first go.

When our protagonist Sheldrake in David Lodge's novel is asked what he actually wants to achieve with his research, the man who never goes on holiday immediately responds: 'to save the world' because 'tourism is wearing out the planet'. He is worried about the conservation of buildings:

> The frescoes in the Sistine Chapel are being damaged by the breath and body-heat of spectators. A hundred and eight people enter Notre Dame every minute: their feet are eroding the floor and the buses that bring them there are rotting the stonework with exhaust fumes. (Lodge, 1991, p. 63)

For us this sounds like one good reason for justifying copysites: they can contribute to the preservation of cultural heritage. In this context, we discuss three examples of exact heritage reproductions, which are not viewed as 'alien' due to their physical vicinity to the original site. The Lascaux caves with their 17,000 years old rock paintings have been closed to the public after fifteen years of exposure to the humidity, body heat and the breathed-out carbon dioxide produced by up to 1200 visitors a day had threatened to ruin the site back in 1963. In 1983 Lascaux II was opened, the first of its kind as an exact replica of the cave at Dordogne, just about 200 metres next to the original. With more than 250,000 visitors a year it has become a tourist magnet which gave reason to the creation of a touring exhibition (Lascaux III) to North-America and Asia as well as the opening of the Centre International d'Art Pariétal – Lascaux IV in Montignac in 2016 (Connexion, 2017).

Similarly, the Chauvet cave, discovered in France in 1994, designated as UNESCO world heritage site in 2014, with rock paintings of an age of more than 30,000 years has never been open to the public. Every Palaeolithic brushstroke was perfectly reproduced thanks to advanced digital technology 3 km away in a 51 million Euro visitor centre that was launched in 2015 (EC, 2016).

Our third example is the famous tomb of pharaoh Tutankhamun, which had rested untouched for more than 3000 years until it was uncovered by the British archaeologist Howard Carter in 1922. Although the tomb in the Valley of the Kings is still open to the public, an exact replica was unveiled in 2012 with the prime goal to protect the original.

The probability that in the near future tourists will be only allowed to visit the replica is very high.

This step provides an outlook on the future of heritage sites in a broader sense. Replicas of fragile sites will become more common. Visitors are becoming more aware of the fact that their presence contributes to the physical degradation at such sites and need to be pleased with the conscience that copies are more sustainable. Based on the experience of the Lascaux caves, the versions two, three and four seem to have more success in terms of visitor numbers due to better accessibility and visibility than the originals ever had.

While tangible heritage sites have been immobile by their very nature, the touring exhibitions or the creation of copysites around the world contribute to the fact that tourists do not need to travel far or frequently. On the contrary, the sites become mobile and seemingly come to the tourists. This phenomenon is even more valid in our modern society which is increasingly based on digital technology. Online 3D museums which are virtually visitable on electronic devices are a further outlook into the creation of copysites of the future and the visitor experiences associated with them.

4. Justifications for visitors at copysites

We deem it important to state that not every tourist is looking for the 'real authentic' experience when visiting a certain destination. It often depends on the opportunity whether an original or a copysite is visited. Just as there seems to be a different reason for the creation of each copysite there are several personal justifications for visitors who are interested in experiencing tangible or intangible replicas. MacCannell has rightly observed that with the global rise of mass tourism the term tourist itself slithered into a crisis and slowly got marked with a pejorative connotation. Etymologically a tourist is someone who goes on a trip and returns to his place of residence. Today, tourists often return also to the same holiday destination and enjoy the vacation as a matter of routine. Consequently, it has become difficult for travellers to have 'authentic' experiences at the same destination every year. Besides, it has become even more difficult to understand what is 'authentic'. Recalling Wang's discussion about existential authenticity, our arguments are in line with the findings that tourists mainly 'seek their own authentic selves' and that whether the visited copysites are authentic is 'less relevant' (1999, p. 366).

Travel motivations can be manifold, in our opinion there is no archetypal tourist such as a 'visitor in a hurry who prefers monuments to human beings' who is concerned with 'the impressions that countries or human beings leave with (him or her), not the countries or the people themselves' as described by Todorov (1994). Silberberg (1995) tries to categorise visitors with his explanation of the different degrees of consumer motivation for cultural tourism. Cohen (1979) argues that there are a range of tourist types seeking varying degrees of authenticity in their travels, while some are motivated by the desire to escape and to engage with the authentic, this is not the case for all tourists (1988). Urry (1990) further distinguishes between the various types of 'gazing' tourists. With the following examples we try to disentangle the dichotomy between the often cited 'good' and 'bad', the 'profound' and 'superficial' visitor, the 'educated' traveller and the 'stupid' tourist as this kind of classification is discussed by Urbain (1991) and Boorstin (1961), among others.

The Chateau Lafitte Hotel, situated in Beijing, China, represents an 'authentic' French Winery and satisfies all visitor expectations with great success. The multi-million dollar replica was realised by Chinese real-estate magnate Zhang Yucheng. The construction of the opulent structure was inspired by his personal fascination for French wine; about 2000 bottles of France's finest are stocked in the private cellar of the residence. The original chateau was designed by French architect François Mansart in 1651 and is located in Maisons-Lafitte, a suburb northwest of Paris. While the chateau in China is obviously a copy, the wine is not. Here we are confronted with the fact that the copysite itself is not acknowledged as the main attraction and so its value of originality is less important. The Chinese visitors are interested in tasting top-wines – such culinary highlights have a better flavour in an 'authentic' ambience and as a result may likewise lead to an increased sale of wine.

As for intangible heritage, for instance, in New Orleans the so-called 'Second Line' performances, celebrated by Afro-Americans, are increasingly performed at hotel lobbies or congress centres for conventioneers. An authentic Second Line would typically take place on a Sunday afternoon when Social Aid and Pleasure Clubs are meandering through the backstreets of the city led by brass bands playing rhythmic up-beat songs and melodies roaring through the public spaces. The club and the band (the first line) are followed by hundreds of residents of the different neighbourhoods (the second line) participating at the street parade. For the entertainment of tourists, though, they are taken off the streets and are reproduced at places where the spectators feel more comfortable (Sakakeeny, 2013). In such staged events the first line remains, the visitors are supposed to substitute the second line.

Also the dance-driven parades of the local 'Mardi Gras Indians' (carried out by black performers masking Indian) with their colourful made-to-measure suits and tambourine guided chants, are continuously commodified within the borders of the tourist-centre of New Orleans. While their traditional events take place far off the commercial hotspot of the city the 'fakelore' reproductions are staged within a few blocks of the architectural heritage of the French Quarter. The tangible context of the heavily marketed Vieux Carré with its renovated and restored ironwork galleries and lace balconies are very important assets for visitors. The tourist-centred performances of Afro- and Native-American cultural heritage just feel more typical and authentic if you experience them in 'original' locations.

As mentioned previously, the provision of health and safety is an important characteristic for copysites since visitors pay attention to security and prefer places where they feel safe. For example, in New Orleans shootings happen regularly at the so-called Second Lines and parades of Mardi Gras Indians that are held somewhere in the backstreets of the Big Easy. Moreover, visitors do not have access to original sites: these Afro-American street-based parades often pop up on improvised occasions, are neither promoted outside the clubs and neighbourhoods nor are they seeking the participation of outsiders. The same happens with the famous jazz funerals – as a tourist it is hard to realise when someone has died for whom a special funeral is organised. The only possible way to participate is when one books a mock jazz funeral including a down-beat playing brass band, a black priest, an empty coffin and a crying widow woman. The question about access is even more complete at the French caves of Chauvet and Lascaux which are closed for the public.

Visitors at copysites are not always attracted by the tangible asset but value the intangible surrounding atmosphere and activities as well. For example, tourists at the

Venetian lagoon in Las Vegas are mainly interested in gambling. At the crystal clear *Canale Grande* they just take their Mediterranean lunch and listen to Italian music. Chinese visitors at the copy-chateau Lafitte Maison are focused on tasting and purchasing French wine, the surrounding architecture just seems to fulfil the function of a nice backdrop. Conventioneers dancing at a mock jazz-funeral or staged second line at a conference hall in New Orleans might interpret the show as a felicitous relief. The city is promoting itself significantly with such parades so the visitors actually expect to make such an experience.

Destination marketing has a major impact on visitor motivation. The tourism authority of Cuba promotes its country with the slogan: *Auténtica Cuba*. The city of Vienna is doing marketing with the wording *Wien hat Kultur* (Vienna has culture). These two slogans implicate that there must be places that are not authentic or that do not have culture – are those destinations meant to be in-authentic or less worth visiting? Are we travelling to Cuba or Vienna because we are convinced that they 'have culture' or are we visiting because the marketing slogans have convinced us that these destinations are worth to be visited since they must be more 'original'?

5. Conclusions

There are arguments that we are somehow obliged to go on holidays where we pretend to be content with our inauthentic experiences, that tourism is performance and routine, that copysites are simply businesses and that originals might be replicas or vice versa: is there something true about Sheldrake's concept that we are not enjoying ourselves when we play tourist?

The attractions of outstanding value (natural, cultural and intangible) remain the archetypes for the cultural tourists: those people for whom culture is an instrument of interpretation and pleasure for the 'real' testimonial of history. Often (but not always) this group of persons coincides with the ones that have the passion and financial resources for realising a travel that is motivated by a specific interest. So here we return to the origins of tourism: spiritual and cultural enrichment, intellectual growth, the shocking beauty of the original (combined with its decadence) and the sum of all experiences that tourism can give us. Should all this be reserved for those travellers who have enough time, money and the sufficient amount of cultural interest?

As travellers, visitors, guests and tourists, we tend to look for extraordinary places and experiences – and copysites sometimes come 'closer to paradise' than the reality if we recall the case of Venice and its *Doppelgänger* in Las Vegas or Eco's observations (1986). At destinations promoting their replicas or staged performances the chance for disappointed visitors is less probable. These places are usually well-organised, catering to specific target groups, the necessary tourist services are present and the consumed experience is what the visitor expected to pay for. Copysites are an example of well-managed tourist places where commodification can show rather positive results. It is the tourism industry and its related businesses that give us the opportunity to visit copysites or enjoy fake performances by providing high quality services. Its visitors have different motivations, needs, interests or opportunities.

Roger Sheldrake's girlfriend broke up their relationship. She said he 'spoiled her holidays, analysing them all the time' (Lodge, 1991, p. 133). In order to stay satisfied during our vacations we may just want to enjoy the moment even though we obviously might not have achieved the ultimate authentic experience.

Notes

1. Sheldrake's arguments appear to come directly from Smith (1977) Hosts and Guests, particularly the chapters by Greenwood 'Culture by the pound' and by Graburn 'Tourism: The Sacred Journey' (1977).
2. The title of this article is influenced by the paper entitled 'Das Kunstwerk im Zeitalter seiner technischen Reproduzierbarkeit' by Benjamin (1936). It is an essay of cultural criticism which proposes that the aura of a work of art is devalued by mechanical reproduction.
3. Source: Statistik Austria 2018.

Disclosure statement

No potential conflict of interest was reported by the authors.

References

Appadurai, A. (Ed.). (1986). *The social life of things. Commodities in cultural perspective*. Cambridge: Cambridge University Press.
Baudrillard, J. (1983). *Simulations*. Cambridge: MIT Press.
Bauer, B. (2014). *Commodification of living cultural heritage in New Orleans. An anthropological case study* (Doctoral dissertation). Retrieved from http://bibliothek.univie.ac.at/

Bauer, B. (2016). Not commodified enough: An anthropological case study about music in New Orleans. In C. Antenhofer, G. Bischof, R. Dupont, & U. Leitner (Eds.), *Cities as multiple landscapes. Investigating the sister cities Innsbruck and New Orleans* (pp. 347–370). Innsbruck: Campus Verlag.

Benjamin, W. (1936). L'œuvre d'art à l'époque de sa reproduction méchanisée [The work of art in the age of mechanical reproduction]. *Zeitschrift für Sozialforschung, 5,* 40–68.

Boorstin, D. (1961). *The image or what happened to the American dream.* Victoria, Australia: Penguin Books.

Bosker, B. (2013). *Original copies: Architectural mimicry in Contemporary China.* Hawai'i: Hawai'i University Press.

Bourdieu, P. (1993). *The field of cultural production: Essays on art and literature.* Cambridge, UK: Polity Press.

Brown, D. (1996). Genuine fakes. In T. Selwyn (Ed.), *The tourist image: Myths and making in tourism* (pp. 33–47). Chichester: Wiley.

Brown, M. (1998). Can culture be copyrighted? *Current Anthropology, 39*(2), 193–222.

Brown, M. (2003). *Who owns native culture?* Cambridge, MA: Harvard University Press.

Burns, P., & Novelli, M. (Eds.). (2006). *Tourism and social identities. Global frameworks and local realities.* Oxford: Elsevier Butterworth-Heinemann.

Canestrini, D. (2001). *Trofei di viaggio: Per un'antropologia dei souvenir.* Torino: Bollati Boringhieri.

Canestrini, D. (2003). *Andare a quel paese. Vademecum del turista responsabile.* Milano: Feltrinelli.

Canestrini, D. (2004). *Non sparate sul turista: Dal turismo blindato al viaggio permeabile.* Torino: Bollati Boringhieri.

Canestrini, D. (2015). Si quieren salvar Barcelona, hagan copias para los turistas. *La Vanguardia.* Retrieved from http://www.lavanguardia.com/lacontra/20150609/54432701638/la-contra-duccio-canestrini.html

Canestrini, D. (2016). Wir müssen draußen bleiben. *Süddeutsche Magazin.* Retrieved from http://www.sueddeutsche.de/reise/staedte-leiden-unter-touristenansturm-wir-muessen-draussen-bleiben-1.3125832?reduced=true

Cohen, E. (1979). A phenomenology of tourist experiences. *Sociology, 13,* 179–201.

Cohen, E. (1988). Authenticity and commoditization in tourism. *ATR, 15,* 371–386.

Comaroff, J., & Comaroff, J. (Eds.). (2009). *Ethnicity, Inc.* Chicago, IL: The University of Chicago Press.

Connexion France. (2017). Lascaux IV sees record visitor numbers despite critics. Retrieved from https://www.connexionfrance.com/French-news/Lascaux-IV-sees-record-visitor-numbers-despite-critics

Eco, U. (1986). *Travels in hyperreality: Essays.* San Diego: Harcourt.

Edensor, T. (2001). Performing tourism, staging tourism. (Re)producing tourist space and practice. *Tourist Studies, 1*(1), 59–81.

European Commission. (2016). Prehistoric cave gets a makeover in the Ardèche, boosting tourism in the Rhône-Alpes. Retrieved from http://ec.europa.eu/regional_policy/en/projects/france/prehistoric-cave-gets-a-makeover-in-the-ardeche-boosting-tourism-in-the-rhone-alpes

Fong, W. (1962). The problem of forgeries in Chinese painting. *Artibus Asiae, 25*(2/3), 95–119.

Friedrich, A. (2017, July 31). Heading to Venice? Don't forget your pollution mask. *The Guardian.* Retrieved from https://www.theguardian.com/environment/2017/jul/31/heading-to-venice-dont-forget-your-pollution-mask

Goffman, E. (1959). *The presentation of self in everyday life.* New York, NY: Doubleday.

Gotham, K. (2007). *Authentic New Orleans. Tourism, culture, and race in the big easy.* New York, NY: New York University Press.

Graburn, N. (1977). Tourism: The sacred journey. In V. Smith (Ed.), *Hosts and guests: The anthropology of tourism* (pp. 21–36). Philadelphia: University of Pennsylvania Press.

Greenwood, D. (1977). Culture by the pound: An anthropological perspective on tourism as cultural commoditization. In V. Smith (Ed.), *Hosts and guests: The anthropology of tourism* (pp. 171–186). Philadelphia: University of Pennsylvania Press. [Revised in 1989, second edition].

Hobasbawm, E., & Ranger, T. (Eds.). (1983). *The invention of tradition.* Cambridge: Cambridge University Press.

Horowitz, J. (2017, August 2). Venice, invaded by tourists, risks becoming 'Disneyland on the Sea'. *The New York Times*. Retrieved from https://www.nytimes.com/2017/08/02/world/europe/venice-italy-tourist-invasion.html?mcubz=0

Kirshenblatt-Gimblett, B. (1998). *Destination culture: Tourism, museums, and heritage*. Berkeley, CA: University of California Press.

de Kloet, J., & Chow, Y. (2017). Shanzai culture, Dafen art, and copyrights. In K. Iwabuchi, E. Tsai, & C. Berry (Eds.), *Routledge Handbook of East Asian popular culture* (pp. 229–241). London: Routledge.

Lanfant, M. (1995). International tourism, internationalization and the challenge to identity. In M. Lanfant, J. Allcock, & E. Bruner (Eds.), *International tourism: Identity and change* (pp. 24–43). London: Sage Publications.

Lanz, A. (2017). Drohnen. Retrieved from https://www.bfhallstatt.at/themen/tourismus/drohnen/

Lodge, D. (1991). *Paradise news*. London: Secker & Warburg.

MacCannell, D. (1973). Staged authenticity: Arrangement of social space in tourist settings. *American Journal of Sociology, 79*(3), 589–603.

MacCannell, D. (1976). *The tourist: A new theory of the leisure class*. Berkeley, CA: University of California Press.

MacEwan, S. (2017). Kleindienst group launches the floating venice – The world's first underwater luxury vessel resort. Retrieved from http://www.thefloatingvenice.com/kleindienst-group-launches-the-floating-venice/

Müller, K. (2018). Drohnen-Einsatz passt nicht allen. Retrieved from https://www.meinbezirk.at/salzkammergut/lokales/drohnen-einsatz-passt-nicht-allen-d2696696.html

Ritzer, G., & Liska, A. (1997). "McDisneyization" and "post-tourism": Complementary perspectives on contemporary tourism. In C. Rojek, & J. Urry (Eds.), *Touring culture* (pp. 96–109). London: Routledge.

Sakakeeny, M. (2013). *Roll with it: Brass bands in the streets of New Orleans*. New York, NY: Duke University Press Books.

Schwartz, H. (1996). *The culture of the copy. Striking likenesses, unreasonable facsimiles*. Cambridge, MA: MIT Press.

Shepherd, R. (2002). Commodification, culture and tourism. *Tourist Studies, 2*(2), 183–201.

Silberberg, T. (1995). Cultural tourism and business opportunities for museums and heritage sites. *Tourism Management, 16*(5), 361–365.

Smith, B. (1988). *Contingencies of value: Alternative perspectives for critical theory*. Cambridge, MA: Harvard University Press.

Smith, V. (Ed.). (1977). *Hosts and guests. The anthropology of tourism*. Philadelphia: University of Pennsylvania Press.

Todorov, T. (1994). *On human diversity: Nationalism, racism, and exoticism in French thought*. Cambridge, MA: Harvard University Press.

Tunbridge, J. E., & Ashworth, G. J. (1996). *Dissonant heritage; The management of the past and a resource in conflict*. Chichester & New York: John Wiley.

UNWTO. (2012). Tourism towards 2030, advance release, 54th meeting of the UNWTO Commission for Europe 9-10 May 2012, Batumi, Georgia. Retrieved from http://cf.cdn.unwto.org/sites/all/files/pdf/2030_global_0.pdf

Urbain, J. D. (1991). *L'idiot du voyage. Histoires de tourists*. Paris: Payot.

Urry, J. (1990). *The tourist gaze: Leisure and travel in contemporary societies*. London: Sage Publications.

Wang, N. (1999). Rethinking authenticity in tourism experience. *Annals of Tourism Research, 26*(2), 349–370.

Wang, N. (2000). *Tourism and modernity: A sociological analysis*. Oxford: Pergamon Press.

Wang, S., & Rowlands, M. (2017). Making and unmaking heritage value in China. In J. Anderson, & H. Geismar (Eds.), *The Routledge companion to cultural property* (pp. 258–276). London: Routledge.

Wong, W. (2013). *Van Gogh on demand. China and the readymade*. Chicago, IL: The University of Chicago Press.

What makes Paris being Paris? Stereotypes, simulacra and tourism imaginaries

Maria Gravari-Barbas

ABSTRACT

Paris imaginaries have served as inspiration for the creation of themed environments for tourism consumption in several parts of the World. These imaginaries are both the origin and the result of a stereotyped image of Paris, strongly attached to the nineteenth century, to the 'Belle Epoque' and to 'Romantic Paris'. From the hotel Paris Las Vegas, to the Ratatouille scenery at Disneyland Paris or to the residential area of Val d'Europe built near Disneyland Paris, Hausmannian Paris has indeed served as the main inspiration for Parisian simulacra all around the World. Our approach consists on of analyzing the « ingredients » of Paris stereotypes as they appear through two main Parisian tourism sceneries: Paris Las Vegas, in Las Vegas, and Ratatouille: L'Aventure Totalement Toquée de Rémy in Disneyland Paris. The paper concludes on a with the quasi-autonomisation of the Parisian tourism imaginaries which are eventually perpetuated through and thanks to the simulacra places built around the World. The paper stresses in particular on the role tourism plays on in the dissemination and perpetuation of these imaginary lands.

1. Imaginaries of Paris. What makes Paris looks like Paris?

The image of a city is the result of a subtle mix of urban landscape features that identifies this landscape *to be* London while this other landscape *is* Paris. The feeling of '*being in Paris*' is based both on iconic monuments and on more common urban ambiance. It both depends on the recognizability of the Eiffel Tower or the Arc de Triomphe and on more 'generic' architecture of the Haussmannian nineteenth-century Buildings or common Parisian architectural details. This feeling obviously depends on one's cultural background, age, sociocultural characteristics or his/her knowledge of Paris. However, the very effectiveness of the storytelling of themed touristic places figuring Paris relies on the fact that the visitor must immediately understand that he or she *is* in Paris. If this does not occur at the very first moment a visitor enters to a Parisian-themed environment, the place irrevocably loses its credibility since it is the feeling of *being* in Paris that gives a meaning to all the components of the project.

When Paris was to be recreated in Disneyland Paris for the *Ratatouille* attraction, the co-director Jan Pinkava faced *exactly* this problem: 'The basic question for us was: "what would Paris look like as a model of Paris?", that is, what are the main things that give the city its unique look?' (Paik, 2007, p. 122).

This paper aims at analyzing the representation of Paris, in Parisian-themed tourist places. From all the complexity of the urban, architectural, human, social, and cultural features of Paris, which ones are in the end selected and reproduced as the quintessential representation of the city?

The text focuses in particular on the ways that tourist locations thematize Paris by recycling the Parisian geographical imaginaries (Bailly, 1993; Bédard, Augustin, & Desnoilles, 2011; Debarbieux, 1995; Gregory, 1994) which have been themselves historically produced with the contribution of tourism. It analyzes the relationship between tourism imaginaries and places as a dialectical one: tourism contributed to the creation of a Parisian imaginary, on which it draws for the creation of themed touristic environments which, in return, contribute to the creation of the tourism imaginary. The paper aims to show that Paris representations in tourist places go beyond the main landmarks such as the Eiffel Tower or the Louvre. They embrace more complex urban realities both material and immaterial. Yet, the imaginaries behind the Parisian-inspired tourist sites still remain geographically and thematically restrictive. They ignore a large part of the urban 'realities' of Paris, which Paris tourism decision-makers wish to disseminate in their effort to incite tourists to go beyond the hyper-touristic urban perimeter and its stereotypical images.

In order to understand the mirrored and dialectical relationship between tourism imaginaries and tourism places the paper analyzes two examples: the hotel-casino Paris Las Vegas, in Las Vegas, Nevada and *Ratatouille: L'Aventure Totalement Toquée de Rémy* in Disneyland Paris. In terms of methodology this research relies on detailed observation of the two tourist attractions (i.e. Paris Las Vegas and la place de Rémy at Disneyland Paris), with, as a backstage, a more general knowledge of other Parisian-themed environments. It draws also on an exhaustive analysis of the daily press, since 2010 for Paris Las Vegas and 2015 for Ratatouille.

2. City thematization: emblems, icons and simulacra

Several examples of Paris-inspired areas have been built all around the world during the past years. Bosker introduced the term of 'Duplitecture' (Bosker, 2013), to describe these architectural copies produced to a huge extent for residential developments in China (Sui, Zhao, & Kong, 2017) or other parts of the world.

Tourism, however, obeys specific rules. Indeed, when the tourism industry decides to 'play' with Paris, the Parisian imaginary is used differently than for residential 'duplitectural' developments. Liberated from the need for an 'orthodox' interpretation of the Paris architecture and urbanism (to which a typical real estate project has to adhere to), tourism venues can interpret the Parisian features with exaggeration, humor and playfulness.

The reproduction of a themed Parisian environment (be it a theme park, hotel or leisure space), seeking to give to the visitors the feeling that they are in Paris, capitalizes on very distinctive elements that are supposed to represent this city. We can arguably say that when an engineer – or an *imagineer* in the case of Disney (Francaviglia, 1995) – recreates a themed Parisian environment, he draws on the most powerful images of the city. Those are city's landmarks, such as Paris' Tour Eiffel. The sole reproduction of this urban emblem creates a mental association with the city in which it is built. Indeed, by a metonymic effect, 'an emblem functions as an icon of the territory. This icon makes it possible to say, like the Eiffel Tower for Paris, not only: this *is in* Paris, but this *is* Paris' (Lussault, 2007, p. 173). Since the beginnings of tourism, some buildings have become 'iconic' and have been closely associated with their territory (Jencks, 2005). Reproduced on different media (postcards, posters, advertising leaflets, etc.) they became territorial emblems, they *imaged* the place in which they were built. The fascination for Paris and the will to be assimilated to this city partially explains the number of reproduced Paris Eiffel towers across the world, such as Hangzhou and Shenzhen (China); Kings Island (Ohio), Kings Dominion (Virginia), Paris (Tennessee), Paris (Texas), Atlanta (Georgia) in USA; or in several themed and leisure parks. This is also the case for other Parisian monuments which have this power of recognizability such as the Arc de Triomphe. In South China Mall, a full-scale reproduction of Arc de Triomphe and the Champs-Elysées aims at recreating, for consumption purposes, the feeling of being in Paris.

If the reproduction of territorial emblems operates a mental association with the city in which the original is reproduced, the immersive experience of a city needs a more holistically themed environment. But how to grasp the ordinary environment of the city, beyond is emblematic landmarks? A team of researchers of Carnegie Mellon, Berkeley, Illinois and the École Normale Supérieure à Paris (Doersch, Singh, Gupta, Sivic, & Efros, 2015) tried to capture the Paris image. The researchers wanted to avoid using the famous landmarks as they appear on Flikr and other photo-sharing websites. As they wanted to offer a more uniform representation of the geographical space, they used the large database of street-level images, captured as panoramas of Google Street View. They worked on 10.000 pictures of Paris available on this data basis, with the goal to define exactly what makes the French capital having this very characteristic and recognizable allure (*idem*), even beyond the Haussmannian architecture that determined much of the urban fabric of the city. The researchers argued that *'the "look and feel" of a city* (in this case, Paris) *rests not so much on the few famous landmarks* (e.g. the Eiffel Tower), *but largely on a set of stylistic elements, the visual minutiae of daily urban life'*. More precisely, 'the top-scoring elements that make Paris look like Paris are the doors, balconies, windows with railings, street signs and special Parisian lampposts' (Doersch, Singh, Gupta, Sivic, & Efros, 2015, p. 106). These features are part of the Parisian 'visual DNA' that has been historically reproduced and disseminated through the arts (cinema, literature or paintings). They are part of a globally shared geographical imaginary of Paris and are even recognizable from those that have never been to Paris.

The staged themed environments of the city, mix emblematic sites and more ordinary elements of Paris. Parises created in various parts of the world are not copies of Paris – none of the reproduced Eiffel Towers has exactly the same size and dimensions than the original; *a fortiori*, none of the recreated portions of Parisian urban areas pretend recreate a 'real' Parisian neighborhood. Distortions of size, forms, analogies or distribution, are common features of all reproduced portions of Paris worldwide. They are not *copies*, but *simulacra*.

According to Jean Baudrillard

Simulation is no longer that of a territory, a referential being, or a substance. It is the generation by models of a real without origin or reality: a hyperreal ... It is no longer a question of imitation, nor duplication, nor even parody. It is a question of substituting the signs of the real for the real. (Baudrillard, 1981, pp. 1–2)

Fredric Jameson (1984) provides a similar definition: The simulacrum's 'peculiar function lies in what Sartre would have called the derealization of the whole surrounding world of everyday reality' (1984, pp. 76–77). Baudrillard claimed that simulacra have become more real than the reality itself. Simulacra stopped being projections of reality, they have become a separate realm of symbols which exist regardless of reality.

Most of the Las Vegas hotel/casinos (New York New York, Paris Las Vegas or the Venetian) are simulacra of the cities they represent (Gottdeiner, 1986). They construct their identities and meanings by using the production methods of the simulacra: while they use their resemblance to the original cities to create an environment of fantasy and theatricality for the consumer, they affirm their own difference from their referent cities (Kaden, 2010). They prevent the consumer from forgetting that they are in the city of Las Vegas, a capitalistic place located in an America city; Las Vegas – neither in Venice nor in Paris.

Paris simulacra rely on sophisticated use of Parisian stereotypes aiming at creating the feeling of 'being there'. The use of these stereotypes is not neutral. It serves the goals of the themed environment (be it a residential area, a commercial shopping mall, a theme park or a hotel) in which it is used (Lukas, 2007a, 2007b). Yet, these environments, be they far from being faithful copies, tend to substitute themselves to the 'real' Paris. They also diffuse a 'Parisian' imaginary to those who visit them – have they already visited Paris or not. Being not *copies*, but *simulacra*, they initiate and introduce parallel fictions of Paris landmarks and neighborhoods, Parisian 'atmosphere' and lifestyle.

According to the geographer Brian Massumi (1987), a simulacrum is a copy of a copy whose relation to the model has become so attenuated that it can no longer properly be said to be a copy. It stands on its own as a copy without a model. Massumi is stating here that, like Baudrillard's assertion, a copy of a copy has lost its connection to the original because it is referring to the copy (Kaden, 2010).

3. Tourism image, imaginaries and stereotypes

Simulacra rely on images and imaginaries. The image of a place is defined by Kotler, Haider, and Rein (1993) as the sum of beliefs, ideals, and impressions people have toward a certain place. Images can be 'open' or 'closed'. According to Avraham

'Open images' are those that enable one to add more characteristics, whereas 'closed images' are those to which one is not likely to add new characteristics, or at least not likely to add characteristics that differ from the core image. (Avraham, 2004, p. 473)

Avraham, names these closed images 'stereotypes': 'simplified attitudes or beliefs about a place that are not examined thoroughly and are difficult to change' (Avraham, 2004, p. 473). A formed stereotype about a place it difficult to change, since this change implies to persuade a large population to be open to a new and different image. Stereotypes are criticized for simplification, essentialism, and uncomplicated design in their representations of other places, people, or things (Lukas, 2016, p. 10). However, stereotypes can be negative or positive. They represent a pool of references which may be used by the designers of themed environments. Those who are fully aware of the value or of the constraining influence of stereotypes can use, and eventually modify, the prevailing touristic models these stereotypes are expressing. However, stereotypes may be problematic for a tourist destination which may wish to go beyond these stereotypes. This is the case for Paris, dominated by stereotypes formed since the beginnings of tourism in the eighteenth or nineteenth century.

Tourism is a dominant creator and disseminator of images, imaginaries and stereotypes. The stereotypical, popular images of Paris have been reproduced, historically, for tourist purposes, on postcards, brochures, Internet sites or blogs. The reproduction of urban environments (be it Paris, New York or Venice), for tourism consumption, is based on the 'essence' of these environments: the common denominator, for a huge amount of people, of what *makes* Paris, New York or Venice. The task of Las Vegas engineers or Disney imagineers is to express this urban 'essence'. According to Francaviglia

> shapers of popular culture like Walt Disney often replicate(d) essences of historical environments (historic architecture and historic landscapes) through a complex process of selection and abstraction of landscape features or elements. Moreover, these elements are often stylized or stereotyped to enhance their effect. Much the same process occurs in the creation of film sets as the visual aspects of place are essential in conveying the 'atmosphere' of both time and place. (Francaviglia, 1995, p. 69)

4. Tourism reproduction of the distinctive elements of Paris as hyperreal expressions of the city

What is the essence of Paris in touristic themed environments? The analysis of Paris Las Vegas and Ratatouille Disneyland aims at analyzing the 'essence of the city' as it is staged in these two touristic popular settings (Figure 1).

4.1. Hotel/Casino Paris Las Vegas: a monumental time-space collision

> Experience everything you love about Paris, right in the heart of Vegas. It's all the passion, excitement, and ambiance of Europe's most romantic city, in the entertainment capital of the world ... Classic style, fine craftsmanship, and authentic details all combine to create Paris Las Vegas' unique ambiance (Hôtel Paris Las Vegas, on live advertisement, 2010).

Hotel Paris Las Vegas is an assemblage of major Parisian iconic sites (Figure 2). Specifically, the Eiffel tower,[1] the Louvre and the Orsay Museums, the Garnier Opera House, the Arc de Triomphe, the Place de la Concorde, the Moulin Rouge are reproduced, most of them finished in a 'Parisian' stone, in the micro-environment which hosts the casino, the restaurants and the other attractions of Paris Las Vegas in front of the main building figured as a 'chateau' with a Mansard roof which hosts the hotel rooms.

These Parisian sites and monuments staged in Las Vegas, are easily recognizable, yet they do not respect the Parisian topography. Dimensions, proportions and distances among buildings are significantly different from the original ones, the indoor and outdoor spaces do not follow an apparent logic, the spatial distribution seems random · ... However, and paradoxically enough, the apparent spatial incongruity of the Eiffel Tower, that crushes down the Opera house, which is next to the Louvre, which contains Montmartre, results to a global narrative about Paris that 'works' despite this time-space distortion: visitors know that they are supposed to be in 'Paris'.

Figure 1. Paris Las Vegas. Monumental collision © MGB, 2009.

This happens despite the fact that Paris Las Vegas does not reproduce (as it is the case for example for the hotel New York New York) a more holistic exterior urban environment. Paris Las Vegas relies on a system of signs and references to Paris landmarks to create a metaphoric image of the city which corresponds to the popular imagery of the city (Brown, Venturi, & Izenour, 1977). For these landmarks,

> it is not necessary for them to be exact copies of their referents, nor do they need to display the age and wear that contains the contextual history of the city, or even a proximity to one another that exists in reality. They signify a new meaning, which says that upon entering the casino or hotel a guest will experience Parisian fantasy unique to the Las Vegas Strip. (Kaden, 2010, p. 41)

To paraphrase Goldberg speaking about another urban-themed hotel, the hotel New York New York

> the real priority of this extraordinary building (…) is to take the image of New York City and wrap it up as tightly and cleanly as an apple in plastic shrink-wrap. And as a piece of packaged

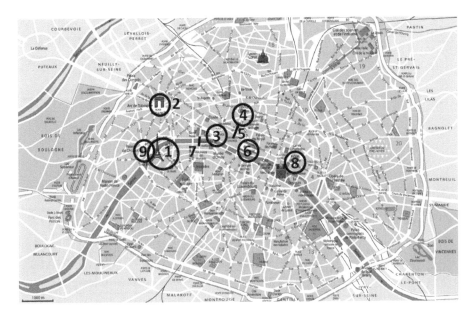

Figure 2. City of Paris. Location of the monuments represented in Paris Las Vegas. 1: Eiffel Tower; 2: Arc de Triomphe; 3: Fontaine des Mers, Place de la Concorde; 4: Opéra; 5: Rue de la Paix; 6: Le Louvre; 7: Pont Alexandre III; 8: Hôtel de Ville; 9: Trocadéro. Elaboration by the author, on Plan Paris 360. https://planparis360.fr/carte-touristique-paris#.WpkU7ejOWuU.

imagery, this hotel has to rank as one of the remarkable moments in recent American architecture. Here is a whole city, turned in a swoop into a theme park. (Goldberger, 1997)

At the same time, the theme-park dimension of the reproduced monuments does not escape the mind of tourists. Some reproduced historical monuments, such as the Arc de Triomphe, representing the Place de l'Etoile, transposes at the hotel context the 'gate function' of an arch. However, its dimensions (2/3 of the size of the Paris Arch), its statuary (which has a lower relief than the original and does not have either any signs of wear or aging) and the lack to any historical reference, prevail the Las Vegas arch from carrying the symbolic, affective and dramatic function of the Parisian monument. In Las Vegas, it becomes another totemic sign of an adjacent casino (Figure 3).

The monuments that were selected to represent Paris are all major tourist attractions in Paris. If the iconicity of these monuments is a key factor for the mental association visitors make between the Paris Las Vegas Hotel and the city of Paris, the presence of a more global landscaping is equally important: it results in creating micro-environments inspired by the most emblematic Parisian urban features – of the Parisian *essence*. The game of the visitor – who visits Paris – who visits Las Vegas, involves indeed the creation of a total environment, offering also the ambiance, the images, the sensations, the tastes, the sounds and smells of the French capital. Hotel Paris Las Vegas does include indeed the elements that make *Paris look like Paris*: Urban furniture (Morris columns, outdoors benches and fountains), boutique windows, café terraces, as well as urban materials (cobblestone streets and sidewalks). Restaurants, bars and cafes of the Paris Las Vegas hotel, with evocative names (i.e. '*Chez Gaby*'), offer food, drinks and services thematically inspired from Paris and France.

Figure 3. Paris Las Vegas. The bistrot terrasse © MGB, 2009.

Indeed, this Paris simulacrum is not only tangible, but also intangible:

> In themed casinos that purport to recreate an actual space, such as a city, the senses are used in a number of ways to connect the worker and patron to an economy of senses that, as simulated as it is, recreates the holistic tableaus of sense that are present in real cities. At the Paris casino, sounds of street performers speaking French mingle with street signs written in the same native language and various French goods in store windows. The smell of crepes and fresh baguettes permeate the Parisian style street outside the casino space, while diners sample French wine on the boulevard that sits against the Strip, just under the recreation of the Eiffel Tower … . (Lukas, 2007c, p. 80)

This 'packaged imagery' works in a normative way. In the same way that the chateau of the Sleeping Beauty in the various Disney parks contains our childhood fairy images (and at the same time represents a set of codes to which we are ultimately very attached and loyal), the Parisian urban environment in Las Vegas seeks to recreate (and therefore *not* to deconstruct) the tourist imaginary of the city. For the hotel Paris Las Vegas, the designers carefully avoided more modern monuments of Paris, such as for example the Centre Pompidou (even if it is an equally iconic, important, visited and recognizable tourist landmark in Paris) because of the incoherence of this modern, high-tech monument with the 'historical' Parisian image.

4.2. *Ratatouille*, « l'aventure Totalement Toquée de rémy », *Disneyland Paris*

« Ratatouille, *l'Aventure Totalement Toquée de Rémy* », opened in July 2014 in Disneyland Paris. For the first time in its history, Disney took the risk opening a major and costly attraction without having testing it before in USA. The attraction was inspired by the 2007 film by Brad Bird which relates the adventures of Remy, a gourmet rat, dreaming to become a chef in a Parisian restaurant.

Rémy is not the first Paris-themed setting made by Disney. The 'world's greatest simulacrum company' (The Economist, 2017) has experience building replicas of Paris. At the EPCOT theme park in Florida, the 'French pavilion' is themed to look like a Parisian neighborhood with a Parisian market (selling French goods), a wine bar, two French restaurants and a small Eiffel Tower.

Paris is also the theme of the near-by residential development of Val d'Europe. Located few kilometers from Disneyland Paris, Val d'Europe is a cluster of imitation *belle époque* housing blocks with mansard roofs inspired by Haussmannian design guidelines. This residential development forms part of the agreement between Disney and the French state made in 1987 to build its European theme park in the area. Disney knows the importance of controlling the land surrounding its parks. In the Paris region, it controls 2230 hectares of Val d'Europe. Val d'Europe shares the principles of 'new urbanism', which promotes mixed zoning, density and walkability (d'Hauteserre, 2013; Picon-Lefebvre, Fabry, & Pradel, 2015). Val d'Europe has been a commercial success. The region's population grew from 5000 in 1989–30,000 in 2016 (about a fifth of working-age adults are employed by Disney). However, some researchers criticized Val d'Europe as a privatized space run by a multinational corporation (Belmessous, 2009) (Figure 4).

After Val d'Europe, the creation of a simulacrum inside the Disney Park seems logical. There is a clear stylistic continuity between Val d'Europe and Ratatouille. Paris, and more precisely Haussmannian Paris, offers the storytelling. According to Laurent Cayuela, show writer at Walt Disney Imagineering, in the Ratatouille attraction 'Paris is not only the setting. It is, with Ratatouille, one of the two main characters of the attraction'.[2]

La Place de Rémy is a simulacrum of the city of Paris. Yet, contrary to the Paris Las Vegas, no major monument of the French capital is represented in the Ratatouille attraction in Disneyland Paris. No Eiffel Tower, nor Triumph Arch or Louvre. Here, Paris, *looks like*

Figure 4. Urban details, Place de Rémy, Disneyland Paris © MGB, 2017.

Paris, only thanks to ordinary architectural elements. If the main attraction of the amusement park is a motion-based trackless 4D dark ride, the main feature is the 'Place de Remy': 'a whimsical new Parisian quarter of the park'[3] an 'atmospheric' Parisian square located 'within an immersive new quarter; a colourful, green, idealised Parisian square with flourishes of Ratatouille magic everywhere and in every detail'.[4]

> The fabulous decor (…) immerses you immediately (…) in a very Parisian atmosphere: an architecture that recalls the Place Dauphine and the Boulevard Haussmann, a fountain inspired by that of the Place des Vosges with its circular basins and its lion heads spilling water, candelabras, the benches and the typical Parisian billboards.[5]

Afterwards, visitors can go straight to the Bistrot Chez Rémy, decorated with giant jar lids for table tops and champagne corks as chairs, to 'give you a rat's view'.

The micro-environment of the Remy's square takes into account the material elements of Paris street life: the sidewalk material and the street pavement, the street furniture, the colors, the boutiques storefronts … Paris references here are close (and are maybe inspired) by the very common characteristics which define the urban fabric of the city, and more precisely the 'visual DNA' as it appears through the compilation of thousands of Google street view database images. The conception of the Place de Remy takes into consideration the 'objective' images of Paris, in their more *basic* expression, the common denominator of 'what makes Paris look like Paris' (Figures 5 and 6).

The attraction represents also the intangible elements of Parisian life. It capitalizes on the stereotypes of Paris, which could be the stereotypical figure of the Parisian *itself*:

> An ice cream seller with an old-fashioned Parisian cart was scooping out free delights, a vibrant flower girl with ditzy hair handed out colorful blooms to passers-by, a mime artist roamed around the square causing mischief, a caricaturist was positioned next to a miniature Parisian street art fair, a silhouette artist cut guests' silhouette from paper.[6]

Guests are also invited to step inside *'Bistrot Chez Rémy'*, a 'Parisian style' table service restaurant and to shop at 'Chez Marianne Souvenirs de Paris'. The collision with the nearby city of Paris is more intense since the Bistrot or the souvenir Shop caters to tourists as 'real' Parisian shops or Bistros. 'Now (…) visitors can feel like they're in Paris without ever stepping foot on the RER train to take them into the city (…). This (…) gives the park something very French, which foreign visitors will love'.[7]

As in other parts of Disney Parks, the spaces are not a copy of a Parisian site, but a simulacrum. However, the inauguration of the Rémy Place, in 10 July 2014 was performed by the then French Minister of Culture, Fleur Pellerin and, few days later, in 17 July 2014, by the Mayor of Paris, Anne Hidalgo … who uncovered the most emblematic feature of Paris, a large blue street sign with the name of the Place de Rémy … in total accordance with the findings of Doersch et al. (2015) about the 'visual essence' of Paris.

5. From tourism simulacra back to the city … the impossible connection?

Recreating the tourist stereotypical imaginaries of Paris, implies that one observes certain codes and respects certain rules; respects the 'norms' and adheres to the spatial stereotypes. The 'ingredients' of the tourist imaginary of Paris as it appears through the Hotel

Figure 5. A Parisien façade, Ratatouille attraction Paris © MGB, 2017.

Paris Las Vegas and Ratatouille, 'crystallize' the Latin quarter, the great monuments, the Bohemian life of Montparnasse and Montmartre, the 'wine and the baguette'.

Tourist reproductions of Paris offer a hyper-real staging based on tourist imaginary long produced by the media, and primarily, cinema. It is difficult not to find similarities between the tourist imaginaries of Paris, as they are represented in Las Vegas or Disneyland Paris, and the filmographic images of Paris (Binh & de Lepinay, 1995). American Filmography in particular (Irma la Douce[8] is an example of a kind) often offers an image of Paris dominated by a set of 'clichés' such as cafés and typical Parisian streets, Haussmannian buildings, Empire Monuments, or *Bel Époque* outdoors furniture. Most recent films (such as *Forget Paris, Moulin Rouge!, French Kiss, Everyone Says I Love You, Midnight in Paris*) continue to depict the French city as the ultimate romantic destination, drawing upon previous films such as *Last Tango in Paris*, *A Little Romance*, and *Paris When it Sizzles* (Kaden, 2010, p. 9). Yet, most of these films have been shot in a studio, in settings that have been designed, ultimately, with the same logic as the rooms, restaurants and the cafés terraces of the Hotel Paris – that is, *to reflect Paris.*

Figure 6. Bistrot Chez Rémy, Ratatouille attraction, Paris © MGB, 2017.

In this sense, not only tourism attractions function as a mirror of a city's imaginary but they often participate in the same image-manipulation performed by the cities them-selves. The attractions appear, therefore, to be a reflection not of the 'real' Paris but of the Paris of tourist imaginary.

In this sense, it would be wrong to consider that Paris-themed attractions are escapist (GUST, 1999), offering imagined, phantasmagorical views of Paris; they are rather reassur-ing. The Ratatouille Parisian square is an example of imagineers' 'architecture of reassur-ance'. As John Hench, one of the emblematic Disney imagineers, put it 'what we are selling is not escapism, but reassurance' John Hench quoted in Gennaway, 2014, p. 66). 'A visit to Disneyland reassures us that things will be okay. Here, everything works, places can be clean, people can be nice, and the pace of the world feels right' (Gennaway, 2014, p. 66).

> Disneyland offered an enriched version of the real world, but not an escapist or an unreal version. We program out all the negative, unwanted elements and program in the positive elements. We've taken and purified the statement, so it says what it was intended to. (John Hench quoted in Gennaway, 2014, p. 66)

Las Vegas and Ratatouille are representative places of an 'architecture of reassurance', an architecture the success of which rests 'in the emotional reassurance they provide (against ...) the constant change of modernity' (Boddy, 2008, p. 279). Several researchers criticized the architecture of reassurance of themed environments. Sharon Zukin (1993) stresses that the main street architecture of reassurance is projected into a coherent land-scape of corporate power. Obviously, these popular, stereotypical images, on which is based the architecture of reassurance, are intrinsically limiting. Most of Paris 'real' life is not reflected. Modern Parisian areas such as La Defense or the 1970s vistas of the front of Seine or the suburbs, are kept away from Paris Las Vegas or from Ratatouille.

Indeed, if the Ratatouille setting is very coherent with the compilation of the Google Street images mentioned before, this is because these most characteristic Parisian features cover only a small part of Paris *[for example, it seems that balconies with cast-iron railings occur predominantly on the large thoroughfares (bd Saint-Michel, bd Saint-Germain, rue de Rivoli].*

The Romantic Paris imaginary, the Haussmann central streets and the *Bel Époque* style embed Parisian simulacra despite the efforts of Parisian tourism and urban stakeholders to offer alternative narratives of the city appealing to young people, repeaters, tourists that want to experience Paris as a festive, creative, modern and off-the-beaten tracks destination. Several initiatives led by city and regional authorities actively try to increase the perimeter visited by tourists, far beyond of the most popular landmarks and neighborhoods, the Haussmannian buildings of the center and the familiar features of Paris as they appear through Google Images or as they are reflected on the imagineers' work.

This 'alternative' Parisian destination exists but has difficulties in developing a tourism imaginary. Or, to put it differently, the stereotypical imaginary of Paris has its own life, in a parallel tourism universe. This Parisian imaginary, separate from the 'real' Paris, exists mainly on the screen or these small replicated Parises build around the world ... and in the minds of (potential) tourists.

6. Conclusion: towards an autonomization of Parisian tourist imaginaries?

Tourism contributes to the multiplication and circulation of Parisian images. It participates in the stereotypical character of these images, which in their turn are used to create touristic themed environments. Yet, these environments tend to become autonomous and to reproduce themselves without referring to the original (i.e. the contemporary, complex, polysemic Parisian metropolis). They contribute to a generic (re)production of an image of Paris: a tourism stereotype. Tourism imaginaries of Paris are not only the result of tourist practices in the 'real city' but also the result of the 'scenic city' created by imagineers. Hotel Paris Las Vegas not only reflects the imaginary, but it also participates in the formation of a Parisian tourism imaginary. Indeed, these Parisian simulacra operate as copies no longer requiring models. Their forms are copies not of their representative cities, New York, Paris, and Venice, but rather, of the popular imagery of these places (Kaden, 2010, p. 15).

It is difficult to conclude on the 'placelessness' of the tourist simulacra (Relph, 1976). The Las Vegas themed casinos or the Disney parks introduced performative parallel spaces. These parallel touristic worlds can be assimilated to the concept of Edward Soja's *Simcity*. The dynamics embedded in *simcities* put in place a subtle form of social and spatial regulation, one that 'literally and figuratively "plays with the mind," manipulating civic consciousness and popular images of city space and urban life to maintain order' (2000, p. 324). 'Order' refers here both as a social order but also as *conformity*.

In this sense, simulacra contribute in maintaining the existence of a disappearing world. While Paris is moving, evolving, changing, Paris Las Vegas or the Place de Rémy in Disneyland Paris contribute into keeping alive not only the nostalgia of a disappearing Paris (Shaw, 2000), but also the urban and social norm to which this narrative is related.

Notes

1. Eiffel Tower in Las Vegas was built at ½ scale in comparison with the original in Paris (165 m high, against 324 for the original, because of the proximity of MacCarran airport which did not allow to build a whole-scale tower as initially the developers wished).
2. Excerpt of the film 'Ratatouille, the making off', Brad Bird, 2007.
3. http://www.dlpguide.com/ratatouille/.
4. http://www.dlpguide.com/ratatouille/.
5. http://monparisjoli.com/2014/07/18/anne-hidalgo-inaugure-la-place-de-remy-a-disneyland-paris/.
6. http://www.dlptoday.com/2014/07/08/ratatouille-the-adventure-at-disneyland-paris-the-complete-grand-opening-report/.
7. http://www.dlptoday.com/2014/06/20/60-reasons-ratatouille-the-adventure-matters-to-disneyland-paris/.
8. Billy Wilder, 1963.

Disclosure statement

No potential conflict of interest was reported by the author.

References

Avraham, E. (2004). Media strategies for improving an unfavorable city image. *Cities, 21*(6), 471–479.

Bailly, A. S. (1993). Spatial imaginary and geography: A plea for the Geography of representations. *GeoJournal, 31*(3), 247–250.

Baudrillard, J. (1981). *Simulacre et Simulation*. Paris: Galilée.

Bédard, M., Augustin, J.-P., & Desnoilles, R. (2011). *L'imaginaire géographique. Perspectives, pratiques et devenirs*. Montréal: PUQ.

Belmessous, H. (2009). *Le Nouveau Bonheur français ou Le Monde selon Disney*. Paris: l'Atalante.

Binh, N. T., & de Lepinay, J.-Y. (1995). Paris. In T. Jousse & T. Paquot (Eds.), *La ville au cinéma* (pp. 519–535). Paris: Cahiers du cinéma.

Boddy, T. (2008). Architecture emblematic: Hardened sites and softened symbols. In S. Michael (Ed.), *Indefensible space. The architecture of the national insecurity state* (pp. 277–304). Abingdon: Routledge.

Bosker, B. (2013). *Original copies: Architectural mimicry in contemporary China*. Honolulu: University of Hawai'i Press.

Brown, D. S., Venturi, R., & Izenour, S. (1977). *Learning from Las Vegas*. Cambridge: The MIT Press.

Debarbieux, B. (1995). Imagination et imaginaire géographiques. In A. Bailly, R. Ferras, & D. Pumain (Eds.), *Encyclopédie de géographie* (pp. 875–888). Paris: Economica.

d'Hauteserre, A.-M. (2013). Les parcs de Disney et la métropolisation de Paris. In M. Gravari-Barbas & E. Fagnoni (Eds.), *Métropolisation et tourisme. Comment el tourisme redessine Paris* (pp. 47–57). Paris: Belin.

Doersch, C., Singh, S., Gupta, A., Sivic, J., & Efros, A. (2015). What makes Paris look like Paris? *Communications of the ACM*, *58*(12), 103–110. Retrieved from https://cacm.acm.org/magazines/2015/12/194622-what-makes-paris-look-like-paris/fulltext#F1

Francaviglia, R. (1995). History after Disney: The Significance of 'imagineered' historical places. *The Public Historian*, *17*(4), 69–74.

Gennaway, S. (2014). *Walt and the promise of progress city*. ThemeParkPress.

Ghent Urban Studies Team. (1999). *The urban condition: Space, community, and self in the contemporary metropolis*. Rotterdam: 010 Publishers.

Goldberger, P. L. (1997, January 15). New York-New York, it's a Las Vegas Town. *New York Times*. Retrieved from http://www.nytimes.com/1997/01/15/nyregion/new-york-new-york-it-s-a-las-vegas-town.html?pagewanted=all

Gottdeiner, M. (1986). *The city and the sign: An introduction to urban semiotics*. New York, NY: Columbia University Press.

Gregory, D. (1994). *Geographical Imaginations*. Cambridge: Blackwell.

Jameson, F. (1984). Postmodernism; or, the cultural logic of late capitalism. *New Left Review*, *146*, 53–92.

Jencks, C. (2005). *The iconic building*. New York, NY: Rizzoli.

Kaden, J. (2010). *Architectural collages. Urban images in Las Vegas hotel/casinos and their production of place*. A Thesis presented to the Faculty of the Graduate School at the University of Missouri-Columbia, under the supervision of Dr. Keith Eggener. Retrieved from https://mospace.umsystem.edu/xmlui/bitstream/handle/10355/9280/research.pdf?sequence=3

Kotler, P., Haider, D. H., & Rein, I. (1993). *Marketing places*. New York, NY: Free Press.

Lukas, S. A. (2007a). How the theme park gets its power: Lived theming, social control, and the themed worker self. In S. A. Lukas (Ed.), *The themed space: Locating culture, nation, and self* (pp. 183–206). Lanham, MD: Lexington Books.

Lukas, S. A. (2007b). The themed space: Locating culture, nation, and self. In S. A. Lukas (Ed.), *The themed space* (pp. 1–22). Lanham, MD: Lexington Books.

Lukas, S. A. (2007c). Theming as a sensory phenomenon. In S. A. Lukas (Ed.), *The themed space: Locating culture, nation, and self* (pp. 75–96). Lanham, MD: Lexington Books.

Lukas, S. A. (Ed.). (2016). *A reader in themed and immersive spaces*. Pittsburgh, PA: Carnegie Mellon ETC Press.

Lussault, M. (2007). *L'homme spatial*. Paris: Seuil.

Massumi, B. (1987). Realer Than Real. *Copyright*, no. 1, 90–97.

Paik, K. (2007). *The art of Ratatouille*. San Francisco, CA: Chronicle Books.

Picon-Lefebvre, V., Fabry, N., & Pradel, B. (2015). *Quand tourisme, loisirs et consommation réécrivent la ville*. Paris: Œil d'Or.

Relph, E. (1976). *Place and placelessness*. London: Pion.

Shaw, C. (2000). *The imagined past: History and nostalgia*. Charlottesville: University Press of Virginia.

Soja, E. (2000). *Postmetropolis: Critical studies of cities and regions*. Oxford: Basil Blackwell.

Sui, D., Zhao, B., & Kong, H. (2017). *The development of copycat towns in China: An analysis of their economic, social, and environmental implications* (Working Paper WP17DS1). Lincoln Institute of Land Policy. Retrieved from https://www.lincolninst.edu/sites/default/files/pubfiles/sui_wp17ds1.pdf

The Economist. (2017). We'll always have Val d'Europe. Disney has built a pseudo-Paris near Paris. Retrieved from https://www.economist.com/news/europe/21725807-worlds-greatest-simulacrum-company-finally-outdoes-itself-disney-has-built-pseudo-paris-near

Zukin, S. (1993). *Landscapes of power*. Berkeley: University of California Press.

Tropical and Eastern Paris: architecture, representation and tourism in Brazil and China

Felipe Loureiro and Roberto Bartholo

ABSTRACT

The article discusses the case of architectural copies to develop a reappraisal of Karsten Harries' [1997. *The Ethical Function of Architecture*. Cambridge: MIT Press] theory of architecture as a representational art. Focusing on examples from contemporary China and nineteenth-century European architecture, it becomes clear that many works of architecture represent and 're-present' other buildings – and that, in some cases, this is the result of an attempt to translate what the 'original' buildings represent. This representational character of architecture is especially significant in the context of tourist experiences. If, as Salvatore Settis [2016. *If Venice dies*. New York: New Vessel Press] argues, cities have a 'body' and a 'soul', both are deeply affected by the huge crowds of contemporary mass-tourism. This phenomenon leads to further analogies between urban disorders and relational pathologies, discussed along the *buberian* dialogical approach: a building can be addressed as an 'it', or a 'Thou', but only in the latter case may this relation demand an effort of translation – and representation. The article closes with a reference to the case of the architectural morphology of the city of Rio de Janeiro – marked by numerous attempts to create 'tropical' translations of other cities, especially Haussmann's Paris –, its tourism patterns and attractions.

Introduction

The aim of this article is to present a way of understanding architecture as an effort of both *representation* and *translation*. This proposition is anchored in a reflection on the experience of buildings in the context of contemporary tourism, where the notions of representation and cross-cultural communication become evident.

If, as Salvatore Settis states (Settis, 2016), cities have a 'body' and a 'soul', it is reasonable to think that both are deeply affected by the presence of huge crowds of tourists. This body/soul analogy allows the development of further analogies between urban disorders and relational pathologies – which are interpreted using the *Buberian* dialogical approach, taking 'I-Thou' and 'I-It' relations as primary relational patterns (Buber, 1937).

The article discusses the case of the Chinese architectural copies built during the last few decades, taking these 'simulacrascapes' (Bosker, 2013) as the starting point for a reappraisal of Karsten Harries' understanding of architecture as a *representational* art (Harries, 1997). Works of architecture represent and 're-present' buildings – made by human hands or nature –, and in doing so shape the world according to the reality of a language, in the sense proposed by Vilém Flusser in his classical book *Língua e Realidade* (Flusser, 2011).[1] Architectural copies are attempts to translate what 'original' buildings represent.

A building approached by the Buberian dialogical approach may be an 'It', or a 'Thou', but only in the latter case this relation may demand an effort of translation. In the case of 'I-It' relations, this effort is dismissed because we, in advance, take for granted that we already have the necessary (instrumental) knowledge required for dealing properly with such building.

The article closes with a reference to the case of the architectural morphology of the city of Rio de Janeiro, forged by a sequence of attempts to create 'tropical' translations of European cities like Lisbon and, especially, Paris.

Body and soul/I and Thou

The tourism industry is one of the biggest and most profitable in the World. However, is it culturally sustainable? Anyone who visits a city like Rome during the vacation season will very likely find the city crowded with tourists, but almost completely devoid of Romans. This may be a seasonal phenomenon in Rome, but it has become a more enduring situation in Venice. In his book *If Venice Dies*, Salvatore Settis describes how the city's population has been rapidly decreasing over the last few decades, and discusses the impacts of this exodus.

According to Settis, every city has a *body* – 'made of walls, buildings, squares, and streets, etc.' – and a *soul* – an 'invisible city' formed not only by the city's inhabitants, but also by 'a tapestry of stories, memories, principles, languages, desires, institutions', etc. (Settis, 2016, pp. 13–14). Even though Venice's body may appear to be preserved, its soul is changing rapidly. Preservation efforts that focus mainly on the body of the city seem to ignore the fact that its soul is also part of what used to attract visitors from all over the world. Whether this is still the case is questionable, since the 'death' of Venice's soul drastically changes the experience of visitors (Edwards, 2017; Giuffrida, 2017).

Venetians are not the only ones afflicted by this kind of 'disease of the soul'. Byung-Chul Han argues that the twentieth century was an 'immunological age' in which the greatest threats were poised by the 'viral violence' of external agents (the most dangerous of all being nuclear weapons). The new millennium forged a new age in which the greatest threats are poised by 'neuronal violence' of internal agents (the most dangerous of all being terrorism) (Han, 2015, pp. 4–7).

To blame the tourism industry or even tourists themselves for this new 'Death in Venice' – or maybe for the death *of* Venice – is an attempt to enclose this phenomenon within the immunological framework of the twentieth century. According to Han, we are currently afflicted not by the negativity brought in by an external agent, but by an excess of positivity: too many stimuli. This excess is in the usual routine of millions of tourists who hop off a cruise ship in Venice and run through the streets following a designated circuit, taking pictures of the most famous buildings and then retreating to their floating hotels – eager to rest from an exhaustive day of 'tourist work'. During this kind of planned, fast-paced visitation, there is no place for meeting the soul of the city, which has been reduced to an object to be captured through (digital) technical images. This rupture is not limited to the experience of the tourist – it becomes a sort of 'neuronal disorder', similar to an identity crisis, to the reality of the city itself.

In his famous book *I and Thou*, Martin Buber states: 'The attitude of man is twofold, in accordance with the twofold nature of the primary words which he speaks' – the combined words 'I-Thou' and 'I-It' (Buber, 1937, p. 3). We can relate in two ways to each and any 'thing' – people, animals, objects: treating it as a 'Thou' or as an 'It'. However, the 'I' that relates to an 'It' is of one kind; the relation to a 'Thou' demands and creates another kind of 'I'.

Following this Buberian perspective, we *experience* the 'It', while we *encounter* a 'Thou' (Buber, 1937). An 'I-Thou' relation is an event, not a product – and thus cannot be planned. According to Buber, 'The Thou meets me. But I step into direct relation with it' – the 'other' only becomes a Thou when I put myself in relation with it, seeking this encounter (Buber, 1937). We usually do not seek this in 'functional' interactions or transactions like that between a client and a cashier, for instance – we are not really engaging with that other person as an 'I', we only have an 'instrumental' relation with 'It'.

As Pedro Abreu argues, the same happens when we relate to an object such as a building or a work of art – we can experience it as an 'It', or put ourselves in the position of having an encounter with it, turning it into a 'Thou' (Abreu, 2007). Fast-paced tourist routes tend to look to monuments and urban spaces as 'Its', as objects to be admired from outside – and photographed, of course. These experiences promote a suppression of otherness – we treat something that could be engaged as a 'Thou' merely as an object, an 'It'. When I deal with an It, I already know what it is and how I should appropriately behave. When I deal with a Thou, I do not. I am open to mutual influence in a meeting and I accept the risks of learning new things that may change my way of being. The new technologies of information and communication open new spaces of experience and horizons of expectations. It is possible to make a virtual visitation of a site before traveling there.

Therefore, the touristic experience may be reduced to a plain confirmation of a knowledge I already have. In Buberian terms, it means that the I-It relation excludes the I-Thou. Or, in Han's diction, the touristic experience is built upon a suppression of otherness. However, this should not mislead us to a condemnation of all I-It relations This would be a mistake, since these relations are surely necessary for human institutions and social life as a whole. The danger is to live in a context shaped exclusively by I-It relations, denying time and place for I-Thou relations.

Abreu and Malheiros (2013) argues that a work of architecture can be defined as a portion of space that allows human beings to be fully human. In other words, it allows the 'I' to become a 'Thou' to itself. This 'psychoanalytical' dimension relates to a notion presented by Gaston Bachelard in his book *Poetics of Space* (1994): our imagination builds images of the spaces we inhabit, and we constantly revisit these images not only when we experience new spaces, but also when we endeavor to engage with 'displaced' reveries. The image is not exactly a memory fixed in the past – it is revived every time we put ourselves into a new encounter with it. We 'dwell' in these images, as Bachelard says (Bachelard, 1994). Going back to Buber, we find that 'The I of the primary word I-It (…) has no present, only the past', since '[t]he present arises only in virtue of the fact that the Thou becomes present' (Buber, 1937, p. 12). When we put ourselves into a direct relation with something, addressing it as Thou, we make it present – even if it is a memory of a long-gone experience.

This presentification reveals a link between identity and memory, something that becomes clear in the example of Alzheimer's disease, in which the deterioration of the individual's memory leads to a deterioration of his or her identity. Again, according to Abreu, the same goes for architecture (Abreu, 2007). A monument, he argues, is an object that invites us to remember; it is the agent of a 'call to remembrance', and it has a memory content – something similar to what Pierre Nora calls a *lieu de memoire*, defined as 'any significant entity, whether material or non-material in nature, which by dint of human will or the work of time has become a symbolic element of the memorial heritage of any community' (Nora, 1996, p. xvii). This memory can become present when the monument is addressed as a Thou; but, if the otherness of the monument is suppressed, it will only be addressed as an 'It' – and this is the basis of the tourist routes we have mentioned before, something Abreu calls 'hyper-modern cultural tourism'. This kind of attitude towards architecture transfers the focus away from local inhabitants and closer to the tourists themselves, who will only have a quick, fleeting encounter – at best – with the building. In the paradigmatic case of Venice, the deterioration of its soul may be causing something like Alzheimer's disease – the city may be losing its memory, and this may eventually cause it to lose its identity.

Architectural copies

This objectification of architecture also seems to be present in the copies of Western architecture built in China over the last few decades. Residential developments all over the country replicate parts of cities like Venice and Paris, trying to attract both dwellers and visitors. These residential neighborhoods are built around monuments that seem to pursue some sort of connection with the Western world. These buildings seem to shock, or at least surprise, most Westerners, and such reactions point to the apparently unambiguous relation between architecture and place – something that becomes obvious when one sees a picture of a Chinese worker carrying a ladder in what seemed to be a photograph of an 'authentic' Austrian village (Hoeller, 2015).

Considering the concepts that we have presented before, we may be led to think that someone who builds a copy of a monument like the Eiffel tower is treating the original building as an 'it', as an object that can be replicated just like an image, regardless of the relationship it has with its surroundings – and this seems to be something that cannot be ignored in the case of works of architecture. However, this phenomenon is more complex than it may seem in a first glance.

The notion of authenticity is at the core of any discussion regarding this phenomenon. These buildings and cities may look 'fake' to the Western eye not only because they feel 'out of place', but because we know of the existence of the model, which we see as the original, the authentic. Bianca Bosker (2013) argues that, for the Chinese, the distinction between the original and the copy is not that clear. Wen Fong clarifies this subject pointing to 'four methods of forging, known in Chinese as: *mu*, to trace; *lin*, to copy; *fang*, to imitate; *tsao*, to invent' (Fong, 1962, p. 102). Each category of copy is judged and valued in specific terms:

- A tracing copy (*mu*) 'aims to produce an exact replica of the original' (Fong, 1962, p. 110);
- A free-hand copy (*lin*) 'is like a wild goose which flies along with its companion. Together, they are like two clouds drifting across the blue sky. Swiftly they glide over ten thousand miles, each coming eventually to rest at a different destination' (Yüeh K'o, *Tan-ch'ien Tsung-lu*; in Fong, 1962, p. 113).
- An adaptation (*fang*) may combine elements from different models, such as an example in which the painting 'is clearly derived from a leaf in an album attributed to Shih-t'ao and dated 1699', while 'the inscription along its top reproduces in smartly sleek strokes, the writing on another leaf of the same 1699 album' (Fong, 1962, pp. 115–116).
- In a pastiche (*tsao*), there is 'a strange feeling of contradiction between the different parts of the picture', which seems to be 'devoid of any true emotion' – 'all the elements have been reduced to bare clichés' (Fong, 1962, pp. 117–118).

Westerners may tend to see all Chinese architectural replicas as pastiches (*tsao*), since they seem to be 'plagued by a strange feeling of contradiction' (Fong, 1962, pp. 117–118). However, as Fong puts it,

> For an art-historian who is interested in the development of painting style, the difference between a *bona-fide* replica and a cleverly-made forgery quickly vanishes, and the all-important question of authenticity seems to lose all its sensational appeal. A well-made copy, regardless of its original intentions, is obviously valuable historically. (Fong, 1962, p. 102)

This value comes from the fact that, in the making of any copy, 'Every "slip" of the hand reflects either a change of the physical circumstances, which may be entirely accidental, or a change of the attitudes of the maker, which, we hope, will be significantly meaningful' (Fong, 1962, p. 102).

Although this attitude towards copies may seem something peculiar to Chinese culture, we can also find similar attitudes in the history of Western architecture. *Le Panthéon*, a popular tourist destination in Paris, is an eighteenth-century building that makes a very direct reference to the 'original, authentic' Pantheon, built in Rome many centuries before. Not too far from this French 'copy', we can find the church of *La Madeleine*, which follows the model of Roman temples such as *La Maison Carrée* in Nimes. However, despite the criticisms made by many modern architects who saw in these buildings mere pastiches of forms copied from the past, they do not seem to shock us as their Chinese counterparts do today.

According to Hillel Schwartz in his book *The Culture of the Copy*, 'The more adept the West has become at the making of copies, the more we have exalted uniqueness. It is within an exuberant world of copies that we arrive at our experience of originality' (Schwartz, 1996, p. 175). The press and the following process of industrialization changed our understanding of what is an original and what is a copy, since, in the case of a mass-produced item, it makes no sense to think in terms of originals and copies – the first item produced is the same as the last; only the *design*, which is in fact abstract, is unique. Many modern architects aimed at introducing this industrial logic into architecture, but this was only partially achieved. Modern, post-modern and contemporary buildings consist of compositions of pre-fabricated standardized elements, but the building itself – the composition – is still unique, just like the design of a chair, a spoon or a car.

However, in the case of architecture, the design is not an idea that lies 'behind' the product; the design has a concrete presence, and this presence turns it into something unique. Even in the case of identical buildings, site-specific relations are usually enough to affirm the uniqueness of each 'block'.

This is probably why a Chinese critic quoted by Fong uses an architectural analogy to describe a copy made by tracing (*mu*):

> To make a tracing is like building a house: even though the beams, the brackets and the rafters all have their strictest measurements, when everything is put together, the spirit and the form (*ch'i-hsiang*) [of each building] will naturally have their own unique merits and faults. (Yüeh K'o, *Tan-ch'ien Tsung-lu*; in Fong, 1962, p. 113)

This uniqueness that is characteristic of architecture may contribute to the notion that we can address a building as a 'Thou', since each person is unique – even in the case of identical twins. Thus, we have no trouble in identifying the church of La Madeleine as a unique building, and not just a copy of a Roman temple.

An example presented by Bosker may signal a similar phenomenon in Chinese culture. Interpreting an essay written by Zong Bing, a fifth century Chinese artist and scholar, Jerome Silbergeld concludes that 'a good simulacrum – one that manages to capture the essence of the original – will be imbued with a "life force", or *qi*, making the sign a perfect substitute for the "original" referent on which the sign is based' (Bosker, 2013). We may say that the simulacrum – in this case, a landscape painting – can present itself as a Thou and provide an image that substitutes the image that could be produced by the encounter with the landscape itself. Thus, both the original and the copy can, according to Bing, be experienced in the same way. If we transfer this notion to the field of architecture, we can say that the church of *La Madeleine* can be addressed as a Thou, and that the encounter with this Thou is not just an encounter with this specific, unique *individual*, but also an encounter with the Roman temples that this individual represents – and *re-presents*. Thus, through its presence, a building such as this can give a visitor a glimpse of centuries of architectural history in a direct, 'personal' way. If the visit does become an 'encounter', the visitor is more likely to regard the building not as something he saw, but as someone he *knew*.

Architecture as representation

According to Bing, painting is a representational art – it aims at recreating the encounter with its subject matter –, and, according to Karsten Harries, this is also the case of architecture. Harries clarifies this notion by quoting Francesco Milizia, an Italian historian from the eighteenth century, for whom architecture was 'an art of imitation, as are all other arts. The only distinction is that some of them have a natural model on which the system of imitation may be based. Such a model architecture lacks, but she has an alternative one offered to her by the natural industry of men when they built their first dwellings' (Harries, 1997, p. 119). Thus, Harries argues, architecture represents buildings – *Le Panthéon* and *La Madeleine*, for instance, which represent their Roman models.

Bringing this notion both to the nineteenth century eclectic architecture of the West and to the contemporary Chinese simulacra, we can understand how '[r]epresenting other architecture, the work (...) re-presents itself in the image of an ideal, thus creating a fiction about itself. By its choice of what to represent and of the form of representation, it communicates a particular understanding of what is taken to matter in architecture, signifying a particular ideal of building and thus of dwelling' (Harries, 1997, p. 120). Thus, *La Madeleine* re-presents an ideal image of the classical temple, while the city of Thames Town, built around Shanghai, re-presents an ideal image of the small English town – sunlight included, for some reason (Herbert, 2012).

As his quoting of Milizia implies, the view proposed by Harries echoes the prevailing view among many eighteenth-century theorists, who believed that the Greek temple was a translation, into stone, of an original building type made of wood. The idea of translation has obvious implications for the dialogue between East and West, and may provide an insight into the essence of the Chinese simulacra.

According to Vilém Flusser, each language not only expresses a different view of reality, but shapes and creates a different reality (Flusser, 2011). He argues that there are at least three 'different types of worlds, in which human intellect lives' (Flusser, 2011, p. 68) – the worlds of inflecting, isolating and agglutinating languages. Most European languages are inflecting languages, in which elements (words) are grouped in situations (phrases); inside the situation, the element 'maintains its identity and steps into a relation with other elements' (Flusser, 2011).

Chinese is an isolating language, which consists of elements (syllables) with no specific meaning, used as pieces for an 'aesthetic whole' formed by mosaics or sets (Flusser, 2011). These sets obey primarily aesthetic rules, not formal, logic rules. Flusser summarizes the difference between inflecting and isolating languages: 'If the ideal of the inflecting phrase is Truth, then the ideal of the syllabical set is Beauty' (Flusser, 2011, p. 72).

Statements about other languages are, at the very best, translations, that is, an effort to approach a limit. Translating, we may come closer, but we never reach the otherness. In this sense, translating is the most important dialogical tool. Chinese architectural copies express an attempt to 'move' or relocate the thoughts (phrases) of the Western world directly to the Chinese context.

The idea of falsification may only apply to the world of inflecting languages, as the Chinese practice of *shanzhai* – the production of counterfeit name-brand goods – may suggest. The eclectic 'revivalist' architecture produced in the West, especially during the nineteenth century, was probably freer in its re-presentation of classical or gothic architecture because there was no fear of falsification. The copies of Western buildings built in China over the past few decades re-present the history of Western architecture in order to represent an ideal of a Western lifestyle and the dominion of Chinese culture over it.

Going back to the case of Venice, we can surely think that the copies of the city – not only in China, but all over the world – do not actually celebrate the original, but banalize it. These copies usually just represent a stereotyped image of the city, providing picturesque sceneries that may lead those who visit the real Venice to see it in the same way – the way promoted by hyper-modern cultural tourism.

On the other hand, we can also see some more positive outcomes of this banalization of the original. Firstly, if the Chinese really cannot see that much of a difference between the original and a well-made copy, maybe millions of Chinese tourists will be satisfied by visiting the Chinese copies, not feeling urged to visit the original – and thus sparing Venice of a huge flow of tourists. Secondly, following on the attempt to look at this phenomenon from a western perspective, we can also think that these copies may even act as a 'backup'. If something happens to Venice – reports that the city may be 'sinking' are not rare –, these copies may give future generations the possibility of experiencing something like 'the lost city of Venice'. In this case, the assimilation of Venice by other cultures could save it – at least partially.

In a less provocative manner, we can learn from Fong's example and at least include these copies into the 'history' of their models – 'In the reconstruction of an ancient master as an artistic and historical individual, copies and imitations of all ages must be treated with equal attention as historical "documents" of different qualifications' (Fong, 1962, p. 102). As an example, we can analyze how European eclectic architecture – which was itself made of 'copies' (*Le Panthéon, La Madeleine, etc.*) – was also copied, usually with the intention of (re)creating a 'civilized' environment that echoed the European model.

Rio de Janeiro as a 'tropical' Paris

This intention was very clear in a number of urban renovations promoted in Latin America from the half of the nineteenth centuryto the first decades of the twentieth century. Most of these projects aimed at copying the overall ambiance of European capitals – mostly Paris, seen as the quintessential model for a civilized, modern city – in order to transform colonial towns into cosmopolitan urban centers. It seemed that, by building capitals following the Parisian model, Latin American countries would include themselves in the pantheon of civilized, modern nations.

The city of Rio de Janeiro, for instance, was founded in 1565, after the Portuguese finally defeated the French invaders who had forged an alliance with the Tupinambá leaders and settled in an island in the Guanabara Bay ten years before. However, the Portuguese occupation was focused on exploring and exporting sugar and *pau-brasil* to Europe, and the region only began to develop after 1763, when the Marquis of Pombal transferred the capital from Salvador de Bahia to Rio de Janeiro, following the discovery of gold in the nearby province of Minas Gerais (Fausto, 1995).

In the early nineteenth century, a unique event gave an abrupt and frantic drive to the development of the city. In 1808, with Portugal facing an inevitable invasion by Napoleon's army, prince regent D. João VI moved the whole Portuguese court to Rio de Janeiro – which then became the capital of the United Kingdom of Portugal, Brazil and the Algarves. In a very short period, the population of the city doubled, from around 50.000 people – before the arrival of the court – to over 100.000 (Fausto, 1995, p. 125).

In order to develop the former colony – now the seat of the imperial crown –, D. João opened the Brazilian ports to international trade, and several public institutions were founded. Shortly after the end of Napoleon's rule in France, D. João promoted the so-called 'French Artistic Mission': French artists were sent to Rio de Janeiro with the mission of establishing the Royal School of Sciences, Arts and Crafts, exerting an enduring influence in Brazilian art and architecture.

The presence of these artists – and of the works of art and architecture that they produced during their 'mission' – aimed to include Rio de Janeiro in the cultural environment of Europe – after all, the city was the capital of a European empire. In the field of architecture and urban design, the urge to replicate the European environment began with the introduction of neoclassicism by Grandjean de Montigny, and culminated in the urban reforms promoted in the beginning of the twentieth century (Villaça, 1999).

The proclamation of the Brazilian Republic in 1889 caused no interruptions in this direct dialogue between Brazilian and European – especially French – architecture. In fact, the young Republic also found, in the 'mimicry' of European buildings and cities, a way to become – or at least appear to be – closer to what was understood as the highest degree of civilization. This becomes evident in the reforms promoted by mayor Francisco Pereira Passos between 1902 and 1906, the most iconic being the construction of the Central Avenue (now Rio Branco Avenue) in downtown Rio. These reforms aimed at transforming Rio into a 'Tropical Paris' (França, 1999), and the Central Avenue was conceived as a *haussmanian* boulevard flanked by *beaux-art* buildings such as the Municipal Theatre and the National Library, which were built on French models that, according to the eclectic style that predominated at the time, were already understood as compositions of elements 'borrowed' from different styles, times and places. The intention to produce a homogenous urban environment was so strong that, when the avenue was opened in 1906, some of its buildings were merely facades with no actual buildings behind them – the priority was to provide the city with a 'French face' (Rocha-Peixoto, 2000), tearing down dozens of blocks built according to the previous model of Portuguese colonial architecture.

The construction of this 'tropical Paris' was the culmination of the process begun in 1808 – the urge to 'transform the village of Rio de Janeiro into the new capital of the Portuguese empire' (Holanda, 2003, p. 150). Architectural copies were used to shape the city of Rio de Janeiro as an extension, or even an 'outpost', of Europe – the urban counterpart of the Portuguese court, still reigning in Portugal, but residing in Brazil. This intention was expressed again in 1908, when a national exhibition – largely built on the eclectic, beaux-Art architecture of Paris – celebrated the 100th anniversary of the opening of the Brazilian ports, and yet again in 1922, when an international exposition celebrated the centenary of the Brazilian independence with a combination of the already established Parisian model and the new trend of neocolonial architecture (Rocha-Peixoto, 2000). The presence of neocolonial buildings aimed to present a local identity built on the foundations laid by the Portuguese, while the eclectic buildings affirmed that Rio was built on the likeness of major European cities.

It was also during the 1920s that organized tourism began to take shape in Brazil, and the focus was also to promote the capital as a modern, cosmopolitan city (Daibert, 2014). However, the overall image of Brazil – and especially Rio – in the imaginary of tourists from all over the world became dominated by a combination of exuberant nature – beaches, hills, forests – and a friendly, welcoming population that celebrates and shares cultural manifestations like music and football (Bartholo, Delamaro, & Badin, 2005; Bartholo, Sansolo, & Bursztyn, 2008). This image was largely built in the post-war period, thanks to the Good Neighbor policy promoted by the Roosevelt administration – and the increasing popularity of 'characters' like Carmen Miranda and Walt Disney's Zé Carioca. In its official website, Rio's tourism authority promotes that 'What Makes Rio Special' is mainly its population, the natural settings – the Tijuca forest, the beaches – and popular culture – samba, caipirinha, feijoada, etc.[2] 'Architecture' is one of the last topics mentioned in this section.

At first, it seems that the main attractions in Rio are essentially the landscape and its people. This is manifest both in scholarly studies and in the way the city is usually marketed by the touristic trade. In his classic book *Raízes do Brasil*, Sérgio Buarque de Holanda subscribes to the notion that 'the Brazilian contribution to civilization will be that of cordiality – we will give the world the "cordial man"' (Holanda, 2003). There is a long academic discussion in Brazilian anthropological and sociological studies focusing on the concept of the *homo cordialis* as a key for the understanding of Brazilian cultural identity, and Holanda states that 'The affability in relationships, hospitality, generosity, and virtues extolled by visiting foreigners are indeed well-defined traits of the Brazilian character' (Holanda, 2003). In his study of the collective psychology of the Brazilian people, Meira Penna builds on the analysis made by Holanda – for whom 'The respect normally manifested by other peoples has its counterpart in Brazil in the desire to establish intimacy' (Holanda, 2003) –, arguing that Brazilians tend to search to create opportunities for I-Thou relationships: 'Eros stablishes a concrete *rapport* (…) since the primordial object of affection is the person of the other' (Meira Penna, 1999, p. 179). Thus, 'Amability, cordiality, interest and attention to the external events related to the activities of "the other"' can be 'the positive side of our national psychological type' (Meira Penna, 1999, p. 182).[3]

In the city of Rio de Janeiro, the opportunities for such encounters are usually open in public spaces – beaches, outdoor bars, football stadiums, parks, etc. The space of the city is permeable to intimate encounters that, in other cities, are usually limited to private spaces. Rio is resilient to become the 'Generic City' described by Koolhaas, who compared it to the contemporary airport – 'all the same' (Koolhaas & Mau, 1995). The fact that the urban space is open to the possibility of encounters makes it difficult to plan – but it is also difficult to 'pasteurize it'.

Some of Rio's *favelas* provide an exemplary case. Many of them are located in sites with impressive scenic beauty, and the peculiar architecture of the *favelas* intertwines this beauty and dense I-Thou relational opportunities. This combination between landscape and people made *favelas* increasingly popular among foreign visitors (Bartholo, Sansolo, & Bursztyn, 2009), spurring the creation of specific tours and guides[4] in which the urban environment of the *favelas* is the main attraction. However, this is basically an 'unplanned' urban form, something that seems to have developed as naturally as the landscape itself, and this unplanned aspect also evokes a sense of authenticity – the *favela* is a place apparently not yet conformed and standardized by global economy. Anyway, the fact that some of the *favelas* have been turned into touristic products may indicate an attempt to reinforce or even replicate this synthesis of the city's main attractions: landscape and people.

It seems, therefore, that the soul of the city is far more appealing than its body – its value being limited to the 'nudity' of natural settings. However, the landscape of Rio is not that natural. The coastline was redesigned by a series of landfills, most of them built from the rubble produced by the demolition of hills that enclosed the center of the colonial city – including the Castelo hill, the site where the city was re-founded in 1567[5] Even the Tijuca forest, one of the biggest urban forests in the world, is somewhat artificial – local species were planted on a site that was previously occupied by a coffee plantation. The body of Rio de Janeiro is a unique composition of natural and made-made structures, combined in such a way that the distinction becomes blurred. However, this unique feature is usually dismissed – and even ignored – not only by tourists, but also by many *cariocas* – those who were born and/or live in Rio. In this sense, Rio may be seen as an opposite of Venice – the focus on the soul of the city may be responsible for the neglect and the resulting defragmentation of its body.

Conclusions

As Buber puts it, the basis of our relations not only to other people, but also to things such as buildings and works of art, is necessarily a kind of *dialogue*. Therefore, the preservation of the body of a building is not enough to preserve it as architecture – it is the possibility of engaging in a dialogue that must be preserved. Dialogues happen between an I and a Thou, and both need to be present for it to emerge.

The Portuguese language may help us in pointing the key issue behind this statement. In Portuguese, the word *presente* has a threefold meaning: it may refer to being present in a place; it may refer to the present time; and it may also refer to a *gift*, something that one offers to others. Dialogical relations can happen between people and buildings, but this requires both to be present in the threefold Portuguese meaning – by being 'there', in the present, offering their presence to others.

In the context of hyper-modern cultural tourism, it is no easy task to experience dialogical relations, since fast-paced, planned visitations encourage an 'I-It' approach. Architecture communicates (non-verbally) through its presence, and simulacra or copies may also be dialogical tools. What matters is the presence of each 'I' and the openness to the other – questions of originality or authenticity must become secondary. After all, there is no such thing as an authentic building, and the dialogue with a copy or simulacra may be more enriching and interesting than marching along a designated course, taking pictures of buildings that were once important for many people, but that may have been turned into mere carcasses – soulless fossils from a distant past.

Comparing the examples of Venice and Rio de Janeiro, it becomes clear that the identity of any city is in a constant development, built on the relationship between its body and its soul. Focusing on just one of these dimensions, we can affect not only the image, but also the experience and even the identity of a city. To preserve architecture is to preserve both the body and the soul of buildings and cities, for the sake of both inhabitants and visitors.

Notes

1. An English translation has been released recently: Flusser, V. (2017). *Language and Reality*, University of Minnesota Press. Translation by Rodrigo Maltez Novaes.
2. http://visit.rio/destaque/o-que-faz-o-rio-especial/.
3. Translation by the authors. Original quotes: 'Eros estabelece um *rapport* concreto, (…) porque o objeto primordial da carga efetiva é a pessoa do próximo' (Meira Penna, 1999, p. 179). 'Amabilidade, cordialidade, interesse e atenção pelos acontecimentos exteriores relacionados com as atividades do "outro"' (…) 'o lado positivo do nosso tipo psicológico nacional' (Meira Penna, 1999, p. 182).
4. For instance, Guia Cultural de Favelas. Retrieved from http://guiaculturaldefavelas.org.br.
5. https://infograficos.oglobo.globo.com/rio/castelo-360o.html.

Disclosure statement

No potential conflict of interest was reported by the authors.

References

Abreu, P. M. (2007). *Palácios da Memória II: A Revelação da Arquitectura. Volume I – Secção Teórica: O Processo de Leitura do Monumento* [Palaces of memory II: The revelation of architecture. Volume I – theoretical section: The processo of reading monuments] (Doctoral dissertation). Faculdade de Arquitectura, Universidade Técnica de Lisboa, Lisbon.

Abreu, P. M., & Malheiros, J. B. (2013). *(An)Estética do Turismo: ou a mediatização do Património* [(An)Aesthetics of tourism: Or the mediatization of heritage]. Paper presented at the Seminário Internacional Espaços culturais e turísticos em países lusófonos. Forum de Ciência e Cultura da UFRJ, Rio de Janeiro, November 22–25, 2011. Lisbon: UFRJ.

Bachelard, G. (1994). *The poetics of space*. Boston, MA: Beacon Press.

Bartholo, R., Delamaro, M. C., & Badin, L. (Orgs.). (2005). *Turismo e Sustentabilidade no Estado do Rio de Janeiro* [Tourism and sustainability in Rio de Janeiro State]. Rio de Janeiro: Garamond.

Bartholo, R., Sansolo, D. G., & Bursztyn, I. (Orgs.). (2008). Tourism for whom? Different paths to development and alternative experiments in Brazil. *Latin American Perspectives, 35*, 103–119.

Bartholo, R., Sansolo, D. G., & Bursztyn, I. (Orgs.). (2009). *Turismo de Base Comunitária: Diversidade de Olhares e Experiências Brasileiras* [Community-based tourism: Diversity of outlooks and Brazilian experiences]. Rio de Janeiro: Letra e Imagem.

Bosker, B. (2013). *Original copies: Architectural mimicry in contemporary China*. Honolulu: University of Hawaii Press.

Buber, M. (1937). *I and Thou*. Edinburgh: T. & T. Clark.

Daibert, A. B. D. (2014, June). *Origens do Turismo Organizado no Rio de Janeiro: A Revista Brasileira de Turismo na década de 20* [Origins of organized tourism in Rio de Janeiro: The Brazilian tourism review in the 20's]. *Revista Rosa dos Ventos, 6*(2), 152–163.

Edwards, C. (2017, July 3). *Venice residents protest against tourist influx (online)*. Retrieved from https://www.thelocal.it/20170703/venice-residents-protest-against-tourist-influx-mass-tourism-mi-novado-via

Fausto, B. (1995). *História do Brasil* [History of Brazil]. Sao Paulo: EdUSP.

Flusser, V. (2011). *Língua e Realidade* [Language and reality]. São Paulo: Annablume.

Flusser, V. (2017). *Language and reality*. Minneapolis: University of Minessota Press.

Fong, W. (1962). The problem of forgeries in Chinese painting, part one. *Artibus Asiae, 25*(2/3), 95–140.

França, J. M. C. (1999). *Literatura e sociedade no Rio de Janeiro oitocentista* [Literature and society in nineteenth-century Rio de Janeiro]. Lisbon: Imprensa Nacional-Casa da Moeda.

Giuffrida, A. (2017, July 23). 'Imagine living with this crap': Tempers in Venice boil over in tourist high season. Retrieved from https://www.theguardian.com/world/2017/jul/23/venice-tempers-boil-over-tourist-high-season

Han, B. C. (2015). *The burnout society*. Stanford, CA: Stanford University Press.

Harries, K. (1997). *The ethical function of architecture*. Cambridge: MIT Press.

Herbert, O. (2012, March 8). *Thames town – An English town in China*. Retrieved from https://plazalondon.wordpress.com/2012/03/08/thames-town-an-english-town-in-china/

Hoeller, S. (2015, August 2). *11 cities that China ripped off from the rest of the world*. Retrieved from http://www.businessinsider.com/cities-china-ripped-off-from-the-rest-of-the-world-2015-7

Holanda, S. B. (Org.). (2003). *História Geral da Civilização Brasileira. Tomo II: O Brasil Monárquico. Volume 3: O Processo de Emancipação* [General history of the Brazilian civilization. Tome II: Monarchical Brazil. Volume 3: The process of emanciption]. Rio de Janeiro: Bertrand Brasil.

Koolhaas, R., & Mau, B. (1995). *S, M, L, XL*. New York, NY: Monacelli Press.

Meira Penna, J. O. (1999). *Em Berço Esplêndido: Ensaios de Psicologia Coletiva Brasileira*. Rio de Janeiro: Topbooks.

Nora, P. (1996). *Realms of memory: The construction of the French past* (Vol. 1). New York, NY: Columbia University Press.

Rocha-Peixoto, G. (2000). Introdução. In J. Czajkowski (Org.), *Guia da Arquitetura Eclética no Rio de Janeiro* [Guide for Eclectical architecture in Rio de Janeiro] (pp. 5–24). Rio de Janeiro: Centro de Arquitetura e Urbanismo.

Schwartz, H. (1996). *The culture of the copy: Striking likenesses, unreasonable facsimiles*. Cambridge: MIT Press.

Settis, S. (2016). *If Venice dies*. New York, NY: New Vessel Press.

Villaça, F. (1999). *Uma contribuição para a história do planejamento urbano no Brasil* [A contribution for the history of urban planning in Brazil]. In C. Deák & S. R. Schiffer (Org.), *O processo de urbanização no Brasil* (pp. 169–243). São Paulo: EdUSP.

Simulacra heritagization: the Minyuan stadium in Wudadao, Tianjin

Lu Yue, Gravari-Barbas Maria and Guinand Sandra

ABSTRACT

Based on the example of the Minyuan Stadium, a 2014 building constructed from scratch on the grounds of the original stadium of Tianjin built in 1926, the paper shows how an architectural simulacrum contributes to blur the line between the real and the fake, historical facts and imaginaries and creates distorted geographies of a reinvented destination in which heritage plays a salient role. This paper is grounded in a qualitative research based on the analysis of official documents, *in situ* observations, and discourses drawn from semi-structured interviews with key stakeholders as well as web-based marketing and advocacy materials. The main interest lies in the critical perspective allowed for mainly how this analysis imbeds features of globalisation in a 'communist' country and State-led capitalist economy imbedded within an architectural simulacrum object.

Introduction

When arriving at the Wudadao district, in Tianjin, a metropolis of almost 15 million inhabitants (in 2014) located 120 km south of Beijing, on the Gulf of Bo Sea, inland from the Yellow Sea, one is struck by the imposing Minyuan Stadium. With its large arcades and its imposing volume, the building strongly contrasts with the scale and the morphological aspects of this tourism destination.

The Minyuan Stadium is located in the Wudadao district, also referred as the 'Western architecture district', part of the 'historic' core of Tianjin. Along with other powers, the British established their concession there in the nineteenth century. The area is mainly composed of modernist – Bauhaus style – villas and apartment buildings. This large district with its lush green trees, gardens, low traffic and density give the visitors and residents a real break from the busy megalopolis (Figure 1).

The actual Minyuan Stadium is a simulacrum constructed from scratch in 2014. The original stadium was built in 1926. Considered an important sports facility, it had since then been rebuilt more than three times (Zhu, 2013). Though the new construction has kept the running track, the rest of the building follows a new 'lifestyle' trend with commercial and leisure functions aimed at capturing visitors, residents and tourists. It hosts various restaurants and cafés, museums, nightclubs, diverse high-end retail shops and temporary

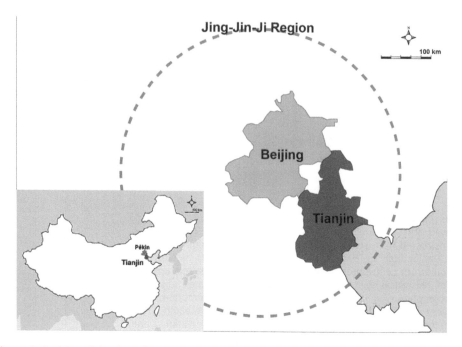

Figure 1. Position of the City of Tianjin in China. Source: Map by Lu Yue, 2017.

events. One can wander around this large building and its arcades at any time as it is conceived as an 'open' public space. Imbedded in the new experiential economy, the place pleases the senses with its design setting and colours lighting at night. If the pastiche architecture of the stadium adopts an indeterminate western style and its oval form takes the initial shape of the stadium built in the same place in the 1920, the building is pure imagination. However completely 'fake' or 'reinvented' it may be, the 'heritage' dimension appears to be an important feature of the project. Its presence alone reminds the visitor or user of an imagined past.

The scope of this paper is to question the stadium's reconstruction under the light of tourism and the experiential economy. One of the main functions of the facility is, according to Yeping Wang, director of Heping District Wudadao Administration Committee, 'to promote the area's cultural diversity and attract an increasing number of foreign tourists' (Bao, 2014). How does this facility respond to tourism and how does tourism, in turn, shape it? What is its narrative and what lies behind it? How do locals respond to the stadium and how does its function and architecture influence and interact with the surrounding environment? We aim to show how this architectural simulacrum does, in fact, contribute to blur the line between the real and the fake, historical facts and imaginaries and create distorted geographies of a reinvented destination in which heritage plays a salient role.

The paper is divided into three parts. First, we will unfold the history of the Wudadao district and trace the stadium's continuous transformation and re-invention during the last decades. Second, we will contextualize the stadium's latest reconstruction within the recent municipal policies aimed at encouraging the development of tourism and the creative economy. This analysis will show that the stadium's last reconstruction breaks with the logic of the previous restorations and/or reconstructions. The simulacrum emergence is directly linked to tourism and creative economy policies. This analysis will stress the essential role the THARD agency played in the district's redevelopment. We will finally set the stadium in the tourism experiential economy, describing the different features it entails and how people interact and behave within its boundaries. We will conclude by giving some critical insights on these types of architectural object explaining why simulacra play a salient role within the tourism economy.

This work is grounded in a qualitative research based on the analysis of official documents, *in situ* observations, and discourses drawn from semi-structured interviews with key stakeholders (translated by Lu Yue) as well as web-based marketing and advocacy materials. The main interest lies in the critical perspective allowed for mainly how this analysis imbeds features of globalisation in a 'communist' country and State-led capitalist economy imbedded within an architectural simulacrum object.

The Minyuan stadium in the context of the Wudadao district

The Wudadao district, which comprises of 130 hectares, 22 streets and more than 2000 buildings, was constructed during the 1920s and 1930s. It represents the main section of the third extension of the British concession, which dates from 1903. Its urban design and morphological setting which today hosts the most affluent population was strongly influenced by the garden city precepts that prevailed in Western countries at the time.

Wudadao was designed as a Western residential quarter equipped with facilities such as schools, churches, parks and playgrounds providing a pleasant and comfortable living environment. Today, the district offers a larger range of functions: housing, education, services such as banks, businesses, trading headquarters, factories and warehouses, churches, entertainment and sports facilities as well as hospitals. The houses were modelled after typical European-styles such as the British, Italian, French, German and Spanish-style. One can also find European classic renaissance and eclectic styles constructions with combinations of Western and Chinese styles. This urban extension gave rise to a first imported model and interpretation of selected features of European style architecture. These architectural interventions are interesting to consider in relation with the concept of 'authenticity regimes' developed by Lucie Morisset (2009). For instance, the idea that heritage produces memories and that heritage production is a cyclical process (Lesaffre Gaëlle, 2009). In the case of the Wudadao district architectural production, the buildings were considered as archetypes or models of interpretations. Yet, it is this Western-inspired archetypical architecture that will later allow them to enter the circle of heritage process. But this reproduction of Western-style architectures will also entail a new storytelling associated with them. It is also the outside gaze (Urry, 1990) from the visitors and their emotional interests in the buildings that will reveal their memories. Today the district entails 443 registered historic buildings (at the city level). For some time, Hong Lu, vice-director of the Bureau of Land Resources and Housing Management of Tianjin Municipality, hoped to have them registered on the UNESCO list (Debelle, 2015, p. 306). The idea has since been forgotten since the two basic requirements for a UNESCO listing (i.e. integrity and authenticity) were not considered as fulfilled by ICOMOS experts (Figure 2).

The original stadium, with a capacity of 18,000 seats, dates from the beginning of the Wudadao district (1926). Several historic events took place there such as the military

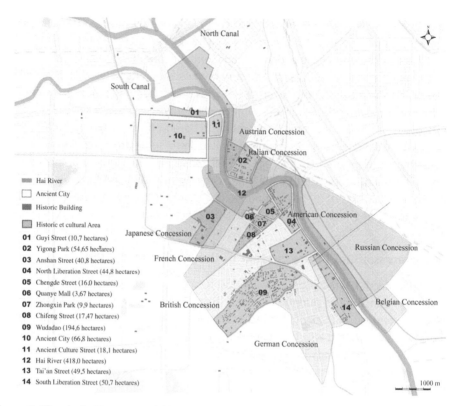

Figure 2. Historic Architecture and Districts in Tianjin. Source: Map by Lu Yue, 2017.

parade to celebrate the coronation of King George VI. The stadium is also associated with legendary stories. For instance, Eric Henry Liddell, a Scottish athlete, winner of the 1924 Olympic Games in Paris and hero of the film 'Chariots of fire', was born in Tianjin in 1902 (1982), is said to have helped with its construction during his stay in Tianjin in 1926 (Magnusson, 1981). Its construction was also associated at the time with the image of one of the major sports facilities in Asia.

The building has since then been rebuilt at least four times (Figure 3). During World War II, it was partially demolished by the Japanese army. In 1943, the British Municipal Committee restored it and reduced its size. After the establishment of the People's Republic of China, grass replaced the clay surface in 1954. The stadium was also fitted with lighting towers. In 1979, following damage in the 1976 earthquake, a second reconstruction took place that was completed in 1982. At this time three-level stands were built which allowed for the accommodation of 20,000 people. After principally hosting soccer games, the stadium closed again for 2 years before reopening in 2014 as a cultural centre. The Minyuan Stadium has been associated with a vicissitude of events during the last ninety years, including wars and rebellions, the devastating Tangshan earthquake and the urban economic development and transition in Tianjin. As a result, the local people, particularly older residents, are very fond of the stadium (Chai, 2015). Its name and associated history, more than its physical appearance, are anchored in people's memory stressing here the importance of the building's immaterial dimension (Figure 4).

Figure 3. Minyuan Stadium. Source: S. Guinand, 2016.

Renovation policies in Wudadao in the context of the urban 'creative' turn

New actors of urban redevelopment in China and Tianjin

From the end of the 1990s to the beginning of 2000s the redevelopment of the Wudadao district was considered as one of the most important works undertaken by city government. These years mostly witnessed the implementation of slum clearance policies such as the destruction and removal of illegal settlements, building renovation, water supplies, gas, heating and the upgrading of public and green spaces (Zhu, 2013, pp. 49–53). Changes in land use also took place and Wudadao progressively evolved from a strictly residential area to a multi-functional site with high-end businesses, residential and tourism features (Wang, 2013, p. 33). It is only with the creation by city government in 2005 of the Tianjin Historic Architecture Restoration and Development Co., Ltd. (THARD) that Wudadao became a place for different creative and tourism project experiments. THARD is a city agency whose main aims are to manage and develop historic districts in Tianjin. In Wudadao, THARD started in 2006 by renovating a group of modern British style buildings of two stories, which it turned into the Minyuan Terrace Cultural Creative Block. The renovated Minyuan Terraces have become, since their opening in 2009 a meeting place for artists, designers and fashionable millennial (Tianjin Municipal Bureau of Land Resources and Housing Administration & Chinese Society of Cultural Relics, Committee on Twentieth-Century Architectural Heritage, 2016, p. 218). One can find cafés, wine and cigars bars, fusion food, as well as art galleries and a museum of traditional Chinese art. The place also hosts different cultural activities (exhibitions, concerts, etc.). This first project mixing creative industry with historic buildings has been promoted as a success

Figure 4. Evolution of the Minyuan Stadium. Source: Association Memory of Tianjin, 2014.

story by city government since visitors can experience 'history' as well as the 'contemporary urban life' (Tianjin Tourism Bureau, 2016) (Figure 5).

Since then, different renovation projects in the Wudadao district have been undertaken by THARD. One example is the Qingwangfu complex, the former house of the last Emperor's uncle, constructed in 1922 and turned into a luxury hotel in 2011. THARD, qualifies it as an 'urban cultural relic club' that has gone under complete renovation. Other examples are the boutique hotel in the Shanyili building, part of the Qingwangfu complex and located at its western edge and the Xiannong Courtyard former residence of the Tientsin Land Investment Co.'s employees, recently transformed into a place for leisure and consumption with franchise stores such as Starbucks, Craft Beer and In & Out. The design framing which insists on the western architectural features of the buildings and the story playing on historical values have set up the Wudadao district as a landscape ready for consumption (Figure 6).

The Chinese government structure and political context give interesting insights on how policies are being carried out more specifically in urban redevelopment projects.

Figure 5. The Minyuan Terrace in Tianjin. Source: Lu Yue, 2016.

Since the beginning of the 1990s, economic development has been decentralised to provincial, municipal and local governments. Chinese cities have become responsible for their own economic development (Henriot, 2015). Municipal authorities organise and manage the city while economic actors take the leadership on urban production (Lin & Wei, 2002, pp. 1537–1538). Chinese local governments are thus the ones carrying real estate and tourist projects. Government bodies (mostly at the county, prefecture, or provincial level) are present as both stakeholders (co-owners) and regulators (Nyiri, 2009, p. 163).

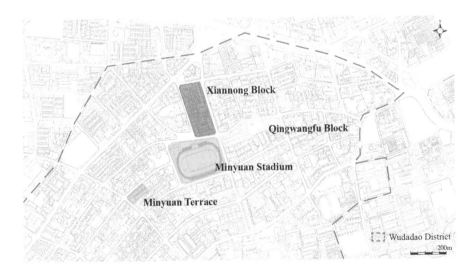

Figure 6. Renovation and tourism projects by THARD in the Wudadao district. Source: http://www. qingwangfu.com/News_22.aspx (February 2017).

In comparison, in France for instance, heritage rehabilitation projects or public infrastruc-tures (mostly projects of general interest) are being led and managed by a *société d'éco-nomie mixte* (SEM) set by local authorities. This structure usually entails a majority of public capital (51– 85%). In China, on the contrary, despite the ostensible 'separation between government and business' (*Zhengqi Fenkai*) carried out in the 1990s, most large tour operators and travel agencies are affiliated with government services and are, as public entities, often run by former or current officials (Nyiri, 2009, p. 163). The same can be said for real estate development.

In Tianjin, the institutional and legal framework established (at the local level) in 2005 for the protection of the city's heritage shows how regulations and operations have been conducted in the city. The power over protection and development of historic buildings in Tianjin remains highly centralized, both administratively and operationally, with local gov-ernment playing a dominant role. The municipality insists on heritage projects that are 'government-led and enterprise-operated' (*Zhengfu zhidao, qiye yunzuo*) in order to achieve the goal of 'high-level planning, restoration, management and utilization' (Lu, 2010, p. 77). Thus, THARD was established as a public enterprise with the full support and capital of the municipal government to 'protect and rationalize the development of historic buildings in Tianjin and to promote economic development' (Lu, 2010, p. 79), in the former concessions. THARD is now helping to acquire and renovate architectural assets of historic values in a protection perspective, setting its own (along with city gov-ernment) interpretation of authenticity and economic and political agenda behind heri-tage restoration. For instance, the agency chooses which heritage rehabilitation operations are to be carried out, which economic and social sites' features are going to be promoted and how it will be carried out. As such, local government and its agencies play an important role in the shaping of the heritage's and tourism's environment and practices. The landscape's evolution and tourism development of the built heritage in Tianjin involve several public actors participating in this meticulous controlled environment.

Tianjin as a tourist destination

In the early 2000s, Tianjin accelerated its tourism development. This was based on the cre-ation of a new urban brand 'Pearl of Bohai, charm of Tianjin' (*Bohai mingzhu, meili Tianjin*), through promotion campaigns by the local government such as 'New Century, New Tianjin, New Landscape' (*Xin shiji, Xin Tianjin, Xin jingguan*). Moreover, the festivities associ-ated with the 600th anniversary of the foundation of the city celebrated in 2004 consider-ably accelerated government officials' awareness of the possible positioning and opportunities of the city as a tourist destination.

The official promotion of the tourist brand 'To see the modern history of China through Tianjin' was based on the planning of twelve defined tourist districts of which nine were located in the downtown area. These areas were identified as historic spaces (former con-cessions), renovated and themed according to archetypes of the national architectural styles. The districts were separated according to functions, architectural and morphologi-cal criteria: for example, the Chinese old town which had been completely destroyed in the early 2000s at the call of modernity principles, was reconstructed as a commercial area full of antique and speciality shops; in the former German concession (the Rhine City) a large luxury hotel was constructed; the former English and French concessions host a commercial area called the Famous Road of Finances; and the Japanese concession was established as a residential area.

The former Italian concession may be one of the most emblematic examples of urban regeneration policies conducted by THARD. It was renovated in 2008 and was presented as the 'Italian scenic district' (*Yishi fengqing qu*), or the Italian business park. In 2009 it was rebranded 'New I-Style Town' (*Xin Yi Jie*), the 'I' referring to Italy (Marinelli, 2010). On the official website of Tianjin's Tourism Bureau, the New I-Style Town is presented by the municipality as 'the only picturesque neighbourhood of Italian style in Asia' and promoted as a successful example of enhancing exotic heritage 'enabling to discover Italy without ever leaving China' (Marinelli, 2013, p. 86). In the area, one can find bars, cafes, and Italian restaurants with names such as 'Venice' or 'Verona'. Tourists, mostly Chinese, can be seen strolling through the streets which welcome an average of 15,000 visitors a day. These different districts have been completely redefined becoming simulacra: spaces reproducing attributes typical of globalized metropolises such as shopping, culture, finance but following a typical Chinese model: each zone is devoted to a single theme or style. Somehow, these redevelopments and redefinition of 'historic' features and what is meant by 'historic centre' represent as a means for Chinese government but also for Chinese visitors to reterritorialize these former exclusive areas. Again, a parallel can be drawn with Morisset´s authenticity regimes (Morisset, 2009) as models and heritage reproductions are being constructed but with completely different narratives accompanying them, giving another interpretation on the relation to time, space and the Other.

The Wudadao district is no exception to the rule. Its renovation appears to be a success story in terms of tourism reception, at least according to the different labels or rankings it has received. In 2003, it was defined as one of the 'ten new landscapes of Tianjin' (*Xin Jinmen shijing*) by local residents and an expert group as the only site to be chosen among the different concessions (Tan, 2004). In 2005, Wudadao was incorporated in the tourism brand 'Experiencing the modern history of China through Tianjin', under the label 'European Continent Flair' (Wang, Liu, & Liu, 2012, p. 105). The increasing number of visitors has fostered the renovation of historic buildings while at the same time contributing to their transformation from residential to catering and retail functions. These interventions have mostly taken part around the Minyuan Stadium. The building also plays as a central point from which tourist activities radiate.

The stadium reinvention: an architectural simulacrum for the new tourism age of Tianjin

After the establishment of the People's Republic of China, the stadium played a key role during the heyday of Tianjin's sport development. Yet, with the city's development, the stadium's functions for competitive sports have faded; the building was not fitted to new sports facility standards. The stadium was abandoned for some time waiting to find a new role in a transition plan. Despite its historic importance in the context of the Wudadao district, the Minyuan Stadium was demolished in 2012, entirely rebuilt and inaugurated in 2014 as a new venue. Following three main principles 'leisure and physical exercise for all, characteristic cultural demonstration, and tourism supporting services', the renovation plan was fully developed. It integrated the stadium's ground levels and an underground floor. The project followed business-led recipes while maintaining the prior architectural appearance. It created a sport-and-leisure park in the city center (UAM City Development Consultancy, 2013). The new stadium, along with the two other commercial facilities, the Minyuan Terrace and Xiannong Block is certainly the most emblematic tourist, leisure and commercial strategy establishment in the Wudadao.

The stadium now houses several recreational, tourist, commercial and 'cultural' functions. It is close to the urban figure of 'flagship' development common in most urban redevelopment projects in Western countries (Gravari-Barbas, Guinand, & Lu, 2016, p. 8) as it operates as an iconic symbol for the district and is a point of convergence for visitors. Most rentals and information booths are in fact found around the stadium. It also hosts the only existing visitors' centre for all the concessions in Tianjin. In the building, one can find several restaurants (breweries, pizzerias, grills) and cafés in the arcades on the ground floor. Part of the upper floor houses the Wudadao Museum accessed by the visitors' centre. Next to it, one can find a museum of precious stones. The existence of a visitors' centre and related services is, in fact, a required condition to apply for the national tourism ranking of AAA (or higher). Government officials saw its presence as a necessary element in order to complete the tourism functions of the area and enhance its attractiveness.

The basement hosts a large parking lot and a supermarket that sells exclusively imported brand products: Italian toothpaste, Portuguese tissues, French cosmetics, cookies and Japanese candies affordable to wealthy clients. Two bars and nightclubs located on the 2nd floor and the external ground floor, the Vic's and the Live Show, contribute to the 'liveliness' of the stadium. Its festival atmosphere is ensured by the diverse activities and sponsored events taking place within its walls or on the grounds outside such as light shows, outdoor exhibits or children drawing workshops. These different functions add to the creation of a real daytime as well as night-time 'destination' in the sector. The stadium is also the venue of several events such as the Davos Summit in 2014 (Figure 7).

The rebuilt stadium proved to be a real commercial success. During the day or at night people of all ages can be found: one can have a walk with the children, have a drink on the restaurant's terrace, do grocery shopping, sit on the stadium's stands, eat, flirt or just rest. According to Yeming Wang, director of the Wudadao administrative committee, the stadium gets approximately 40,000 visitors per day, a number that can go up to 70,000–80,000 during holidays (Bao, 2014). It also became the major tourist sight of the

Figure 7. The Minyuan Stadium day and night. Source: M. Gravari-Barbas, 2016.

Wudadao district. The example of the Minyuan Stadium also shows how boundaries between tourists and locals have become increasingly blurred (Bock, 2015; Condevaux, Djament-Tran, & Gravari-Barbas, 2016) and how tourism activities are blending with local ones at risk of gentrification (Gravari-Barbas & Guinand, 2017). In this sense, the Minyuan stadium is 'authentic' as it offers local life activities.

The international functions and products of the stadium's image aim at attracting national visitors, as Wudadao, and more generally Tianjin, remain a national tourism destination. The new stadium corresponds to a new generation of shopping centres, which can be depicted as 'lifestyle centres' (Chai, 2015). Unlike more traditional shopping complexes, 'lifestyle centres' rely on a fun component and a huge offer of restaurants, leisure facilities and events. Here, the historic element is important: heritage participates to the attractiveness of the place by bringing a storytelling that brings cultural capital to the place and offering different emotional and memories investments.

Conclusions

The Minyuan case is interesting in demonstrating the role tourism and leisure play in the context of contemporary globalised metropolises. The tangible heritage component of Minyuan Stadium is non-existent since the contemporary idealized stadium was built from scratch. Yet, Minyuan Stadium capitalizes on eighty years of history, its location on the original grounds of the 'historical' stadium and on the perceived authenticity of the Wudadao historic district. 'Western style', as a condensation of the archetypal image of the Wudadao British precinct's architectural codes and styles, imbues the stadium's appearance and features. The location on the same grounds of the original stadium gives undoubtedly legitimacy to the new project. But, contrary to other 'heritage' projects in Tianjin, such as the Pu Yi house,[1] Minyuan it is not a copy – since the stadium never existed in its current shape.

Where the concept of heritage clearly finds here its limits, the concept of simulacrum can be helpful to understand the recent evolutions of Chinese urban space in the context of globalisation. Baudrillard (1981) uses the concepts of the simulacrum – a copy without an original – to explain the development of the postmodern 'to the extent [the simulacrum] addresses the concept of mass reproduction and reproducibility that characterizes our electronic media culture'. According to the author, simulacrum is not a copy (it is not an image with resemblance). It is an image *without* resemblance. The simulacrum is not just a degraded copy. It carries autonomy, which interrupts the relation between the original and the copy.

The Minyuan Stadium is a trans-temporal simulacrum built on an historic location and carrying an historic name. As for Pop Art, such as Andy Warhol's Campbell's Soup Can prints, the stadium 'copy' is pushed so far that it becomes a simulacrum, an image without resemblance with the original building or its successive restorations but in which intangible features seem to become ever more salient.

The layers of history on which the new stadium builds could be secondary for another kind of infrastructure such as a hospital, a school, or office buildings. But for the stadium's tourist-leisure function, history becomes central since it makes part of the stadium's experiential offer. Tourism development in Tianjin and in China, in general, relies on historic and heritage references, but does not always carries the possibility, the means, the will or the cultural framework to do so in classic heritage terms. Tourism produces, therefore, simulacra and goes even beyond, by introducing hyperreal frames, which, overloaded with simulations and images, blur the boundaries between reality and representation, between authenticity and fake, between copies and simulacra.

Note

1. The former residence of Pu Yi, the Last Emperor of China, recently restored, is one of the main tourist attractions in Tianjin.

Disclosure statement

No potential conflict of interest was reported by the authors.

References

Association Memory of Tianjin. (2014, November). 民园简史图说 [A Brief History of Tianjin Minyuan]. 风物 [City Dairy], 34–39.

Bao W. X. (2014, September 9). Revitalized stadium to boost culture and tourism. *China Daily*. Retrieved from http://www.chinadaily.com.cn/regional/2014-09/10/content_18572929.htm

Baudrillard, J. (1981). *Simulacre et Simulation [Simulacrum and simulation]*. Paris: Galilée.

Bock K. (2015). The Changing Nature of city tourism and its possible Implications for the Future cities. *European Journal of Futures Research*, *3*(20). doi:10.1007/s40309-015-0078-5

Chai L. (2015, January). *Minyuan stadium retail area: An emerging retail destination, Tianjin property insight*. Retrieved from https://www.businesstianjin.com/index.php?option=com_content&view=article&id=10772%3Areal-estate-tianjin-retail-market-bigger-and-better-more-about-experience-less-about-shoppingminyuan-stadium-retail-area&catid=217%3A2015-february&Itemid=100

Condevaux A., Djament-Tran G. & Gravari-Barbas M. (2016). Before and after tourism(s): The trajectories of tourist destinations and the role of actors involved in "Off-The-Beaten-Track Tourism": A literature review. *Via@*, *1*(9). Retrieved from http://viatourismreview.com/2016/10/avantetaprestourisme-analysebiblio/

Debelle D. (2015). Les nouvelles dynamiques du tourisme et de la patrimonialisation en Chine: étude des anciennes concessions et du quartier français de Tianjin en particulier [*New dynamics of tourism and heritageization in China: study of former concessions and the French neighborhood in Tianjin in particular*] (Unpublished doctoral dissertation). University of Paris 1 Pantheon-Sorbonne, Paris.

Gaëlle, L. (2009). Lucie k. Morisset, Des régimes d'authenticité: Essai sur la mémoire patrimoniale [Lucie K. Morisset, regimes of authenticity: Essay on the heritage memory]. *Culture & Musées*, *14*(1), 185–187.

Gravari-Barbas, M., & Guinand, S. (2017). Addressing tourism-gentrification processes in contemporary metropolises. In M. Gravari-Barbas & S. Guinand (Eds.), *Tourism and gentrification in contemporary metropolises: International perspectives* (pp. 1–21). London: Routledge.

Gravari-Barbas, M., Guinand, S. & Lu, Y. (2016). Tianjin, de l'ancienne à la nouvelle mondialisation. Continuités et ruptures [*Tianjin, from the old to the new globalization: Continuities and breaks*]. Travel diary of the mission in Tianjin for the research project of the ANR "Patrimondialisation". Unpublished manuscript. Retrieved from https://f.hypotheses.org/wp-content/blogs.dir/3052/files/2016/09/Carnets-de-voyage-Tianjin.pdf

Henriot, C. (2015). Les politiques chinoises de villes nouvelles: Trajectoire et ajustements de l'action publique urbaine à Shanghai [Chinese policies of new cities: Trajectory and adjustments of urban public action in Shanghai]. *Géocarrefour*, *90*(1), 27–38.

Lin, G. C. S., & Wei, Y. H. D. (2002). China's restless urban landscapes 1: New challenges for theoretical reconstruction. *Environment and Planning A*, *34*(9), 1535–1544. doi:10.1068/a3409ed

Lu, H. (2010). 天津历史风貌建筑可持续保护利用探索 [Studies on the sustainable protection and utilization of historic heritage in Tianjin]. 中国房地产 [China Real Estate], n° 1, 77–80.

Magnusson, S. (1981). *The Flying Scotsman: A Biography*. New York, NY: Quartet Books.

Marinelli, M. (2010). The 'New I-Style Town': From Italian concession to commercial attraction. *China Heritage Quarterly*, n° 21. Retrieved from http://www.chinaheritagequarterly.org/editorial.php?issue=021

Marinelli, M. (2013). The Triumph of the uncanny Italians and Italian architecture in Tianjin. *Cultural Studies Review*, *2*(19), 70–98.

Morisset, L. (2009). *Des regimes d'authenticité. Essai sur la mémoire patrimoniale [Regimes of authenticity: Essay on the heritage memory]*. Quebec: Presses de l'Univesrité de Québec.

Nyiri, P. (2009). Between encouragement and control: Tourism, modernity and discipline in China. In T. Winter, P. Teo, & T. C. Chang (Eds.), *Asia on tour : Exploring the rise of Asian tourism* (pp. 153–169). New York, NY: Routledge.

Tan, R. W. (2004). 天津地名考 津门十景史话 [Study on place names in Tianjin, history of ten new landscapes of Tianjin]. Retrieved from http://news.sina.com.cn/c/2004-04-20/00383145033.shtml

Tianjin Municipal Bureau of Land Resources and Housing Administration & Chinese Society of Cultural Relics, Committee on Twentieth-Century Architectural Heritage. (2016). 问津寻道 [A glimpse of Tianjin: An appreciation of historic architecture protection]. Tianjin: Tianjin daxue chubanshe.

Tianjin Tourism Bureau. (2016). 老房子里开出想象的花儿 [The imagination in the old house]. Retrieved from http://chn.tjtour.cn/tianjin-chpc/travelDaren/superiorView.action?superiorProgramId=8a9a2b3558af0a9a0158b3b287590012

UAM City Development Consultancy. (2013). 天津市民园体育场及周边地区保护与发展专项策划 [Special planning for the protection and the development of the Minyuan stadium and its surrounding areas]. Retrieved from http://www.uamchina.com/news_111.aspx

Urry, J. (1990). *The tourist gaze: Leisure and travel in contemporary societies*. London: Sage.

Wang, S. (2013). 天津五大道历史文化街区保护性旅游开发研究 [Studies on the protective touristification of the Wudadao historic and cultural district in Tianjin] (Unpublished master's thesis). Shaanxi Normal University, Xi'an.

Wang, Q. S., Liu, T. & Liu, W. L. (2012). 天津 "五大道" 主题街区旅游开发对策 [Strategies for the Touristification of the Wudadao District in Tianjin]. 当代旅游 (Tourism Today), n° 4, 104–106.

Zhu, X. M. (2013). 中国.天津.五大道: 历史文化街区保护与更新规划研究 [wudadao, Tianjin, China: Conservation and regeneration of historic area]. Nanjing: Jiangsu kexue jishu chubanshe.

Seeing is believing: miniature and gigantic architectural models of second temple

Yael Padan

ABSTRACT

Miniature architectural models are often used as signs or markers, which frame a touristic site as a place worth visiting. In this paper I explore the relations of such models to the 'real' sites, as well as to other copies and representations. The article examines the Holyland Model, a miniature model showing Jerusalem in the year 66 AD, which has become a tourist site in its own right. The central building in this model is the miniature Jewish Temple, which was later replicated in both miniature and gigantic copies. I follow the transformation of this Temple image, from a secular-cultural symbol of Israeli national identity to a represention of different Orthodox Jewish and Christian evangelical agendas. I argue that the large-scale buildings in fact replicate the miniature models, inverting both sign relation and scale relation between original and copy. The use and manipulation of the image of a building, produced initially at the Holyland Model, has become an essential device for the production of meaning and affect.

Introduction

This paper examines architectural models and their relation to their referent full-scale buildings. Miniature models are cultural material artifacts, used in order to present the visitors with specific versions and interpretations of the exterior world. For the tourist, miniature models represent the toured country, or some of its highlights, in a condensed spatial and temporal form. They mark sites as tourist attractions, which are then recognized by the visitors. Importantly, the process of recognition is essential in order for the tourist to make sense of the touristic experience.

Miniature representations act as 'off-site markers', which frame the 'real' sites as original or authentic (MacCannell, 1976, pp. 111–117). The authentic sites must be marked and differentiated using representations, because authenticity is a sign relation (Culler, 1988, p. 160). However, I will argue that the relation between 'marker' and 'real site' is more complex. To discuss this relation I will use Max Black's definition of a model as a three dimensional, more or less true to scale, representations of an existing or imagined material object (Black, 1962, p. 219). Following this definition, I will question the point in which a model becomes a building,

considering its scale, its representational qualities, and to what extent it has an independent existence of its source object.

The four cases that I examine include two miniature models of the Jewish Second
Temple, located in Jerusalem, which were produced as markers of the absent ancient
shrine: The Holyland Model, and the Temple Model at Aish HaTorah Yeshiva. The two
other models of the Temple are large-scale buildings: the Great Temple at Florida's Holy
Land Experience is a scaled-down version of the 'original' Temple; and Solomon's
Temple at Sao Paulo, Brazil, is even larger than the original. My argument is that the
large-scale buildings in fact replicate the miniature models, inverting both sign relation
and scale relation between original and copy. They raise questions concerning scale
and representation: what is the relation of miniature representations to the full-sized referent? How do large-scale buildings replicate their models? Can these buildings then be
termed models?

To answer these questions I refer to Bill Brown's *Thing Theory*. Brown suggests that we
look through objects, or take them habitually for granted. He argues that objects turn into
'things' when they cannot pass unnoticed. This can happen when objects disfunction,
break down or stop working, causing a shift in our perception: 'The story of objects assert-
ing themselves as things, [...] is the story of a changed relation to the human subject and
thus the story of how the thing really names less an object than a particular subject-object
relation' (Brown, 2001, p. 4). Further, Brown argues that 'things' are 'what is excessive in
objects', and can be imagined as 'what exceeds their mere materialization as objects or
their mere utilization as objects – their force as a sensous presence or as a metaphysical
presence, the magic by which objects become values, fetishes, idols and totems'
(Brown, 2001, p. 5).

Throughout this article I will suggest that miniature models refer to external 'objects',
and by doing so, they assert themselves as 'things'. By posing the visitor in front of a miniature version of a building, scale relations are inverted: rather than being dwarfed by a
building, the visitor is empowered over its miniature. The habitual subject-object (or
body-building) relations are changed. The model is recognizable as a reference to a
specific full-scale building, but it does not function as a space that encloses the body.
Brown emphasizes 'the simultaneity of the object\thing dialectic, and the fact that, all at
once, *the thing seems to name the object just as it is even as it names some thing else*'
(Brown, 2001, p. 5, original emphasis). The model names the building, but it also names
itself as a separate entity, which is both a marker of the 'real' site (the building, 'object')
and an artifact ('thing'). Indeed, in the cases explored in this article, the full-scale buildings
gain their state of 'thingness' because they are replicas of the miniature object\thing. Thus
both the miniature and the full-scale buildings inspired by it, all mark and indicate the
ancient Temple as 'real'.

The article concludes by comparing the qualities of miniature and gigantic Temple representations, and the ways in which scale is used as a tool in communicating narratives of
collective identity, belonging, and 'geopiety'. The term 'geopiety' was used by Tuan (1976)
to describe human attachment to place, and later by Long to indicate 'that curious mix of
romantic imagination, historical rectitude, and attachment to physical space' (Long, 2003,
p. 1). I will examine the power of these replications to construct both physical and imagined realities, and to produce and re-produce meaning and affect.

The Holyland Model[1]

The Holyland Model (Figure 1) is a miniature model (scaled 1:50) of ancient Jerusalem, designed and built between 1962 and 1966, on the grounds of the Holyland Hotel in Jerusalem. It represents Jerusalem at the time of the Jewish Second Temple, in the year 66 AD, when the city was at its greatest geographic extent and at a high point of Jewish independence, shortly before its destruction by the Romans in 70 AD (Tsafrir, 2009, p. 9). This period is of central importance in the Zionist ethos, which emphasizes its connection to symbols of national independence during biblical times (Liebman & Don-Yehiya, 1983, p. 37). It is also significant for Christians, as the time and city of Jesus. The Holyland Model is a well-known site in Israel and has been widely studied.[2]

At the time of the model's construction, Jerusalem was divided by a border, drawn following the 1948 war. Most of the city's historical and holy sites, located in and around the Old City, were under Jordanian rule, and Israelis had no access to them. This geo-political situation had detrimental effects on the city's economy and particularly on the sector of tourism. Indeed, the Holyland Hotel was one of the only hotels built in Israeli West Jerusalem around this period (Cohen-Hattab & Shoval, 2015, pp. 118–119).

The founder and owner of the Holyland Hotel, Hans Kroch, wanted a cultural and tourist attraction for his hotel, which was located quite a distance away from any particular site of interest. He decided to commission the model, which was to form 'a link between the magnificent Jerusalem of the past and Jerusalem of today' (Ribon, 1965). Kroch was concerned about West Jerusalem, which was cut off from its ancient origins and historic monuments: 'We are missing what Rome and Athens have – ancient buildings', he told a journalist in 1965 (Ribon, 1965). Kroch decided to recreate the missing historical sites in the model. His declarations echoed the secular Zionist narrative that goes back to

Figure 1. The Holyland Model at the Israel Museum, Jerusalem, with the Temple in the foreground. Photo: Yael Padan.

Second Temple in linking the Jews to the territory of contemporary Israel. He is quoted as saying: 'if Jews cannot get to the holy places, the holy places will come to them' (Cherni & Tsafrir, 2009, p. 14).

Kroch approached Professor Michael Avi-Yonah, a scholar of classical archaeology at the Hebrew University, who specialized in the period of the Second Temple, and asked him to design the model (Tsafrir, 2009, p. 9). His wife Hava Avi-Yonah, an artist, made the working drawings. Planning the model was a complicated task, since Michael Avi-Yonah decided to show the city in its entirety, even if this meant compromising scientific accuracy (Tsafrir, 2009, p. 12). Since there was no access to the sites, the design had to rely on earlier excavations, ancient texts, Jewish sources and the New Testament (Cohen Hattab & Kerber, 2004, p. 67), and on Hellenistic and Roman archaeological sites around the Mediterranean (Lavie, 1964; H. Avi-Yonah, personal interview, February 24 2010).

One of the central features of the Holyland Model is its appeal to the visitors as authentic and accurate. Although it is a creative representation rather than an original object, it has always had a reputation of a scientific and authoritative reconstruction of ancient Jerusalem. As a representation of archaeology, it is part of the legacy of archaeology in Jerusalem, which is closely connected to the political context. The modern archaeological study of Jerusalem (initially led by Protestant scholars), has been used over the past two centuries as a tool to pursue and to demonstrate 'essences' of origin, as well as national roots (Silberman, 2001, p. 501).

The model was intended to provide its visitors with a sense of identity and meaning, by constructing a link between people, country and history. Its miniature geography of remains played a part in representing the modern nation as a continuous existence in time and space, using the past as a source of common history and collective memory. Moreover, the Holyland Model also gave shape to a longing for Jerusalem's future unification.

This longing was fulfilled when Israel conquered the Old City and East Jerusalem in the 1967 war, and the ancient sites became accessible to the national collective. In this new context, the Holyland Model retained its significance as a popular site, because paradoxically its representation of the entire ancient city is easier to comprehend than the actual ruins that were excavated on site.

In 2006 the grandson of Kroch, now the owner of Holyland Tourism Company, decided to make new development and construction plans for the site. The Holyland Hotel was demolished, and the model was relocated to the Israel Museum (Figure 2). This is the largest museum in Israel, located in Jerusalem next to the parliament and government buildings. It houses some archaeological artefacts, which date back around the time represented in the model. The relocation of the Holyland Model from the hotel to the context of the Israel Museum has greatly enhanced its status as both a national exhibit and a scientifically accurate representation (Padan, 2017a; Chapter Three).

Due to its reputation as an authoritative reconstruction of ancient Jerusalem, the Holyland Model, and particularly its Temple building, has inspired the construction and exhibition of many other Temple models, both miniature and full-sized. In the following sections, three of these models will be discussed.

Figure 2. The Holyland Model at the Israel Museum, Aerial view. Photo: ©The Israel Museum, Jerusalem, by SKY BALLOONS.

The temple model at Aish HaTorah Yeshiva[3]

The model on the roof of Aish HaTorah Yeshiva is one of several recent Temple models located in different institutes operating in Jerusalem,[4] and influenced by the Holyland Model. Balakirsky Katz suggests that the proliferation of such models has to do with the relocation of the Holyland Model. She argues that the move to the Israel Museum has altered the model's meaning for Orthodox Jews: whereas in the context of the hotel, they perceived the model as a recreation of a Jewish religious site, the move to the museum had changed its meaning into an Israeli cultural object (Balakirsky Katz, 2011, pp. 355–6). She points out that some Orthodox religious leaders reject the museum, not merely because it displays non-religious art, but also because it reflects a secular approach to Jewish identity in terms of culture rather than religion. For these leaders, the museum cannot house the Temple, since they perceive the Temple itself as the shrine that should house the Jewish treasures (Balakirsky Katz, 2011, p. 358).

The relocation of the model therfore influenced the decision of Orthodox institutions to commission and display other models of Second Temple. Within such institutions, the Temple models are viewed in a context that focuses on the centrality and authority of religion in Jewish national life. Religion, rather than culture, is viewed as defining the Jewish State (Balakirsky Katz, 2011, pp. 357–8).

The model at Aish HaTorah Yeshiva (Figure 3) was commissioned from Michael Osanis, who had built two smaller Temple models previously. His first model was inspired by a

Figure 3. The Second Temple Model on the roof of Aish HaTorah Yeshiva, Jerusalem. Photo: Anat Padan.

dream, which he described in a newspaper interview. In his dream, Osanis looked into the past and saw the ancient Second Temple, and then glimpsed into the future:

> Behind the horizon that heavenly light shone all over the sky. [...] I understood this is the light of the next Temple, which is not so far from today. I came to the conclusion: I must pass on what I have been shown (Bruckner, 2010).

Having no previous experience in model building, Osanis spent six months building his first Temple model. Rabbi Israel Ariel, head of the Temple Institute,[5] was impressed by the model and commissioned Osanis to build another larger and more detailed one. This led to the commission of a third model from Osanis, this time by Aish HaTorah Yeshiva, in 2009.

This model, at a scale of 1:60, was placed on the roof terrace of Aish HaTorah Yeshiva in the Old City of Jerusalem. There, the model is viewed with the Muslim Shrines on the Temple Mount in the background. It faces the historic location of the ancient Second Temple on the Temple Mount. Its position suggests the model and – by extension – its source-object, as a tangible alternative to the mosques. Indeed, Osanis perceives it as a step towards the rebuilding of the Third Temple (Bruckner, 2010).

The differences in context and location between the Holyland Model and the model at Aish HaTorah Yeshiva exemplify a shift in the use of Temple models. While the Holyland Model represents secular interest in archaeology as a link to modern Israeli cultural and national identity, its replications represent a view in which the Temple is a symbol for Jewish sovereignty over the Holy Land, part of an ethnonational project (Persico, 2017,

p. 115), which includes a religious search for spiritual, halachic, nationalist or messianic sentiments (Be'er, 2013, p. 24).

I have argued previously (Padan, 2017b) that the Aish HaTorah model is therefore perceived in the context of the religious and political nationalist sentiments surrounding the Temple Mount and the Temple itself in contemporary Israel. As argued by Persico, the merging of political nationalism and religious messianic thought threatens to undermine the Zionist project of secular nationality and democracy: 'it is the end point of Zionism – the point at which Zionism self-destructs' (Persico, 2017, p. 113). I suggest that the model at Aish HaTorah Yeshiva, wiewed with the Mosques in the background, offers a material representation of this possibility.

Aish HaTorah Yeshiva presents the model as a didactic tool, explaining that 'This model helps people envision what it was like to be here at the time of the Temple' (Simmons, 2010). It thus tries to avoid the sensitive political and religious issue of the Temple Mount. But this issue cannot be avoided, as seen in photos of the model on the Aish.com website in a section called 'Today's Israel Photo', showing various sites and scenes from Israel. One photo of the model is captioned: 'Third Temple Model' (http://www.aish.com/photos/326207281.html?s=srcon). Another photo of the model has this text: 'A beautiful replica of the Holy Temple on the rooftop of the Aish World Center, overlooking the real spot of the Temple, may it be rebuilt soon in our days!' (http://www.aish.com/photos/?date=Tammuz_18).

The temple model at the Holy Land Experience

A religious interest in the Temple and a messianic longing for its rebuilding is also central to evangelical Christianity. It is evident at the Holy Land Experience in Orlando, Florida (Figure 4). This site, described on its website as a 'living biblical museum' (https://www.

Figure 4. The Holy Land Experience, map of the park (https://holylandexperience.com/park-map-directions/).

holylandexperience.com/about/), seeks to combine a physical and spiritual experience using lage-scale replicas of sites from ancient Jerusalem, including the Second Temple:

> It is a living, biblical museum that takes you 7000 miles away and 2000 years back in time to the land of the Bible. Its combination of sights, sounds, and tastes will stimulate your senses and blend together to create a spectacular new experience.

> But above all, beyond the fun and excitement, we hope that you will see God and His Word exalted and that you will be encouraged in your search for enduring truth and the ultimate meaning of life. (https://holylandexperience.com/about/)

The Holy land Experience (HLE) was initiated by Marvin Rosenthal, a Jew who had converted to Christianity as a teenager and became a minister in 1968 (Spalding, 2002, p. 14). He is the founder of Zion's Hope, Inc., a Christian ministry active in converting Jews, which initiated the HLE as a non-profit evangelical ministry. On the website of Zion's Hope (http://www.zionshope.org), its aim is clearly stated:

> Zion's Hope seeks to graciously proclaim to the Jewish people their need for personal salvation through Jesus the Messiah and to proclaim the gospel of the Lord Jesus Christ to all men regardless of race, religion, gender, education, or national origin.

In 1989 Rosenthal purchased a 15-acre site in Orlando, situated next to world famous theme parks such as Disney World and Universal Studios. His vision for the site, as stated on the HLE website, was to 'proclaim the Gospel to as many people as possible; and to help believers have a better understanding of the Judaistic roots out of which Christianity grew'(https://holylandexperience.com/history/).

The vision was realized at an investment of $16 million. The park was designed and constructed by ITEC Entertainment Corporation, whose projects include theme parks, rides and shows, resorts and entertainment centers. As explained on the ITEC website: 'visitors of themed environments seek experiences that excite their senses and enrich their lives beyond imagination. ITEC meets those challenges by turning dream-level concepts into real facilities and experiences' (http://www.itec.com).

The park's opening in 2001 aroused protests from local Jewish leaders (Usborne, 2001). The Jewish Defense League described Rosenthal as a 'soul snatcher' and protested against 'the spiritual destruction of the Jewish people' (Brabant, 2001).

In 2007 the Holy Land Experience was purchased by the Christian Trinity Broadcasting Network (TBN), which currently owns and runs it.

Within and around the sites replicated in the park, dramatic performances and musicals are staged; the buildings provide a backdrop or house the productions. The HLE website (https://holylandexperience.com/about/) declares:

> Recreations of the ministry of Jesus, stories from the Old Testament, miracles and triumphs, and the story of musical praise through the ages will all move your spirit and emotions in praise to our Lord God.

The performances and the spaces both shape the performance-viewing experience for the visitors (Stevenson, 2013, p. 98). Rather than mere entertainment, these are powerful religious tools. As argued by Stevenson:

> Evangelical dramaturgy tries to situate the physical encounter between object/event/space and believer as central to religious meaning-making. In doing so, the re-representation

reinforces evangelical theology, in particular the notion of direct access to an incarnate divine presence (Stevenson, 2013, p. 39).

By moving within the spaces and attending live shows the visitor creates an experience of a personal journey or pilgrimage. This experience differs from the detached overall view experienced at the miniature models discussed previously. Here the models engulf and affect the body: 'From the moment you pass through the gates of our walled city, you will be immersed in ancient Jerusalem.' (https://holylandexperience.com/about/). The abstracted journey is therefore based on the experience of the moving body traveling through space and time. The authenticity of this imagined landscape is achieved by simulating the 'original' building materials, described on the HLE website:

> Then at the grand entrance to the Temple Plaza, walk under a massive archway and behold the gleaming white stone plaza surrounding you with its thirty Roman columns crowned with gold capitals. All this grandeur majestically frames the imposing Great Temple, the place held in highest reverence among the Jewish people (https://holylandexperience.com/about/).

The Temple is indeed a dominant feature of the park (Figure 5). The website further explains that this structure is a half-size scale model which provides 'an accurate depiction of Herod's Temple'. Although this is a scaled-down model, it is large enough to be an imposing. Inside is an auditorium called 'The Theater of Life', where a video outlines human history from the viewpoint of evangelical Christianity. Outside the building, Christian dramas are performed daily, with the Temple and its entrance court framing the scenes (Branham, 2008, p. 24).

As argued by Wharton, the centrality and size of this Temple is indicative of the Temple's place in evangelical eschatology, as well as of evangelical Christianity's

Figure 5. The Holy Land Experience: the Great Temple (https://holylandexperience.com/exhibit/the-great-temple/).

commitment to the construction of a new Temple (Wharton, 2006, pp. 224–225). Is it a building, or a model? Its size certainly indicates that this is no miniature model. Nevertheless, it draws its meaning from a source-object, and it is a scaled-down version; both of these features characterize models.

Another feature of models is their temporal reference: some represent buildings that existed in the past, while others represent contemporary buildings or envision (in the present) future buildings yet to be built. The Temple model at HLE allows the visitors to journey back to ancient Jerusalem, but also offers a vision of the future by representing the restored Jewish Temple (Stevenson, 2013, p. 54). Indeed, this future Temple is the same Third Temple that Michael Osanis aspires to build.

Solomon's Temple, Sao Paulo, Brazil

Solomon's Temple houses the headquarters of the Universal Church Kingdom of God (UCKG). This megachurch (Figure 6) has 10,000 seats, and includes within its 74,000 sqm complex many other functions: a Bible School with classrooms for 1300 children, offices, television and radio studios, and apartments for the priests and for the founder and leader of UCKG, Bishop Edir Macedo. The building is much larger than the 'original' ancient Jerusalem Temple. It took four years to build, at a cost of about $300 million (Romero, 2014), and was inaugurated in July 2014.

In an interview with him on the UCKG blog in 2012 (http://uckg-templeofsolomon. blogspot.co.uk), Macedo explained that a visit to Jerusalem had inspired him to build a

Figure 6. Solomon's Temple, Sao Paulo. Photograph: Vitor Mazuco (https://commons.wikimedia.org/wiki/File:Templo_de_Salomão__1.JPG#globalusag).

Temple in Sao Paulo, which would provide a spiritual experience to its visitors by imitating the Jewish Temple:

> The Temple of Solomon could be built – its replica – here in Sao Paulo. The people could have access to a historic place, extremely spiritual, because it's where God manifested himself, we could say physically, to all the people and Children of Israel in that time.

Blurring the differences between the ancient Temple ('a historic place' from 'that time') and its replica, makes the new Temple a spiritual place, like its referent. Its 55-meter high façade is clad with Jerusalem stone, imported from Israel, thus symbolically importing part of the holy land to Sao Paolo. As noted by Macedo in a televised service, the stones are 'just like the ones that were used to build the temple in Israel; stones that were witnesses to the powers of God, 2,000 ago. The outside will be exactly the same as that which was built in Jerusalem.' (Quoted in Philips, 2010).

The size and appearance of Solomon's Temple serve not only spiritual aims, but also express some wider changes taking place with the growing influence of evangelical Christianity. As argued by Casanova, Pentecostalism (of which UCKG is a branch), is a highly decentralized religion, with no historical links to tradition and no territorial roots or identity (Casanova, 2001, p. 434). I suggest that Solomon's Temple, which is visually linked with the Old Testament and Judaism, is meant to provide a tangible symbol of tradition and territory.

Latin America, which was formerly a Catholic territory, has become a world center of Pentecostal Christianity, and the number of believers has grown rapidly in the past 40 years (Casanova, 2001, p. 437). It is estimated that in Brazil numbers have grown from 5% of the population in 1970, to 22% of Brazil's 200-million population in 2014 (Watts, 2014). Using TV and radio channels (such as Rede Record, owned by Macedo, which is the second largest TV company in Brazil), these churches have gained significant political power and influence. The UCKG, which was founded in 1977, had 1.8 million members in Brazil by 2010 (Romero, 2014). Solomon's Temple positions it as a leading congregation within Brazil's evangelical Christian population.

In spite of the imported building materials, the Sao Paulo Temple differs considerably from the ancient Temple which was built by King Solomon in 960 BC and destroyed in 587 BC (Reiter, 2001, p. 7). There are no physical remains of this temple, but Morrison argues that the Sao Paolo Temple bears no resemblance to the Biblical descriptions, dimensions or details of Solomon's Temple. Thus, neither the external structure nor the interior of the Biblical Temple of Solomon is replicated in Sao Paolo (Morrison, 2013, pp. 1–3). Solomon's Temple at Sao Paolo was designed by architect Rogerio Silva de Araujo, and the UCKG blog (http://uckg-templeofsolomon.blogspot.co.uk), explains the planning considerations:

> Redisigning the King Solomon Temple from the Bible quotations became a big challenge – from the time we had the initial understanding that the scale used by Solomon would not meet the need of the UCKG for today. Moreover, at that time, only the priests could attend it, but this has not applied to the Temple we are building, seen that not only church members but also anyone interested may have the opportunity to go back in time and learn a little more of this amazing project.

Furthermore, Macedo had described the Jerusalem stones as referring 2000 years back, and this was the time of Second Temple built by King Herod (begun 19 BC), rather than of King Solomon's First Temple. Morrison therefore maintains that the Sao Paulo

Temple replicates Herod's Temple (Morrison, 2013, p. 3). Indeed, I argue that the Sao Paolo Temple resembles the Holyland Model's Second Temple.

What is the reason for this resemblance? Arguably, there are more images available of Herod's Temple than of Solomon's Temple, making its replication an easier task (Abascal, 2014). Morrison suggests further reasons:

> The architecture of Herod's Temple was grander, richer and larger than the Biblical description of Temple of Solomon. However, Herod had a reputation as a corrupt and ruthless tyrant who murdered his rivals [...] On the other hand, Solomon and his Temple symbolize wisdom, justice and piety. Bishop Macedo does not mention Herod and only refers to the Temple of Jerusalem or the Temple of Solomon and he makes no distinguish between the two. By writing the narrative of the Temple of Solomon into the architecture of Herod, Bishop Macedo achieves an image of the grand architectural history of Herod whilst claiming the political and the religion legacy of King Solomon. (Morrison, 2013, pp. 5–6).

Consequently, in media coverage of the building process and inauguration of the Sao Paolo Temple, the name 'Solomon's Temple' (referring to the First Temple) is becoming associated with the image of Herod's Temple (which is the Second Temple, built about six hundred years after the destruction of Solomon's Temple). As a result, these two distinct Temples are becoming merged in the public imagination (Morrison, 2013, p. 4).

As I suggested above, the Sao Paolo Temple replicates the Holyland Model Temple, but rather than being a miniature model (as in Aish HaTorah Yeshiva), or a scaled-down model/building (as in HLE), it is much larger than Herod's Temple. Can it be termed a model? Considering Max Black's definition of a model, the Sao Paolo temple is a three dimensional, more or less true to scale, representation of an existing or imagined material object. In fact, its meaning depends on its referent object – the miniature Holyland Model, whose meaning in turn depends on its claim to accurately represent Herod's Temple.

Discussion: the miniature and the gigantic

Going back to Brown's *Thing Theory*, I define the miniature Holyland Model Temple as a transitional 'thing', which not only represents the historic object, but also inspires its translation back into a building. As seen here, aspirations to rebuild the Temple are evident both in Jewish messianic actions, and in the Christian sites discussed.

The larger replications of the Temple thus go a step closer to the original, by simulating its reconstruction as a building. They materialize a vision, that precedes an anticipated building, using the image of the ancient one. This simultaneous reference to the past and to the future characterizes 'things', as defined by Brown: 'Temporalized as the before and after of the object, thingness amounts to a latency (the not yet formed or the not yet formable) and to an excess (what remains physically or metaphysically irreducible to objects)' (Brown, 2001, p. 5).

Scale and its relation to the body is a dominant feature in both the miniature and the gigantic replications. Stewart points out that our means to understand scale was traditionally the human body, and that 'the domain of immediate lived experience' can only take place in the space occupied by the body (Stewart, 1993, p. 101). This determines the relation of the body to both the miniature and the gigantic: 'The miniature allows us only visual access to surface and texture; it does not allow movement through space. Inversely, the gigantic envelopes us, but is inaccessible to lived experience' (Stewart,

1993, p. 102). Stewart further argues that the miniature moves from our hand, which can hold it, to our eye, to abstraction and distancing. The gigantic, on the other hand, 'moves from the occupation of the body's immediate space to transcendence (a transcendence which allows the eye only imperfect and partial vision) to abstraction' (Stewart, 1993, p. 102). I suggest that indeed both the miniature and the gigantic replicas of the Temple discussed here exemplify this notion of distancing from the body and moving towards the abstraction of ideologies, prophecies and visions.

The HLE Temple is large in relation to the body, and even more so in comparison to the miniature model that inspired it. But it nevertheless retains close resemblance, and derives meaning, from the miniature Holyland Model. The HLE Temple is therefore both an exaggerated copy of the Holyland Model, as well as a large-scale (but still miniature) model of the ancient Herod's Temple. Its significance lies in referencing both structures, and this is emphasized by its location within a theme park, a genre in which buildings are replicated in order to create the themed setting. Further, as argued by Stevenson, the theme-park configuration is essential because it is a recognizable and friendly genre:

> Visitors to HLE are prompted to live in a theme park\Christian Holy Land blend that is easy to use, contemporary and, with its Disney-like features, in some respects uniquely American. Their experience navigating and using this familiar, accessible Holy Land constructs an intimate script that is comfortable, comforting and pertinent. And, like all intimate scripts, it serves to verify the certainty of particular beliefs, in this case the crucial, inviolable importance of Christianity to the Holy Land (Stevenson, 2013, p. 118).

At the HLE, both the miniature and the gigantic are present, since the park also includes a miniature model of the entire first-century city of Jerusalem. Like the HLE Temple, this model is also reminiscent of the Holyland Model. Unlike the imagined landscape of the park, which is composed of select replicas irrespective of the 'real' geography, this model provides the physical context by giving an overview of Herod's Jerusalem:

> Visit our model, the largest indoor replica in the world, and see where Jesus walked, ministered, healed, and performed other miracles. Marvel at the massive Temple where the sacrifices took place. Follow the steps that Jesus took from the Upper Room to Calvary and the empty tomb. Enjoy the historical presentation of this ancient city by one of our knowledgeable lecturers. Admire the hand-crafted, life-like figurines, and feel almost as if you are in the city itself (HLE website: https://holylandexperience.com/exhibit/jerusalem-model-a-d-66/).

While the Holylnd Model shows the entire platform surrounding the Temple, at the HLE some of the Temple Mount has been modified. In place of its southern part there is a lowered area where guides stand while explaining the model. Wharton points out that this part of the platform, which was left out, is in the location of today's al-Aksa Mosque (Wharton, 2006, p. 225).

Whereas the miniature is grasped as a whole, the gigantic can only be seen in its entirety from a distance. It is experienced in fragments and parts, exposed one by one, introducing a temporal dimension (Stewart, 1993, p. 79). The architect of Solomon's Temple, Rogério Araújo, has declared: 'We sought to build a colossus, something that would make people stop and gaze, and that's what we delivered.' (Quoted in Romero, 2014). Araújo added a theological explanation for the size of the building: 'We made a larger project in reference to the passage of Haggai, Chapter 2.9, which says, "The glory of this latter house shall be greater than the one of the former'" (Quoted in Abascal, 2014). Nevertheless, the Universal Church website stresses: 'This project is only a replica, not the third temple.' (http://web.universal.org/usa/temple-of-solomon-gods-altar-on-earth/).

Rather, Solomon's Temple is characterized by features of contemporary megachurches: Protestant affiliation, immense size, modern appeal and technological sophistication, which create a powerful devotional experience (Stevenson, 2013, pp. 225–226). Such churches typically have amphitheater tiered seating, large projection screens, and sound systems, allowing church leaders to 'craft precise sensual encounters for worshippers' (Stevenson, 2013, p. 185). I argue that at Solomon's Temple this experience is enhanced by using the image of (Herod's) Temple, established at the Holyland Model. The discourse of the relation between the church and the Temple of Jerusalem prepares the visitor to enter a holy space, which symbolizes historical continuity and a link with the Jewish roots of Christianity, as well as a longing for the rebuilding of the Temple that will bring about the coming of the Messiah (Wharton, 2006, p. 223).

The Sao Paulo Temple has inspired a video artwork made by artist Yael Bartana, entitled 'Inferno', which was shown in the 31st Bienal de Sao Paolo in 2014. It visualizes the inauguration of Solomon's Temple with a grand ceremony, followed by its destruction. 'Inferno' recalls the short existence of Herod's Temple, destroyed by the Romans less than a decade after its completion. The impact of Solomon's Temple on the artist is explained in the exhibition guide:

> On a visit to the construction site of what would become the third version of Solomon's Temple – this time in Sao Paulo – Bartana could envision no other possible future than the prophetic repetition of the past – in other words, its destruction. In what she calls a 'pre-enacting', the artist documents, between the forgetting and celebration of a fantasized past, the way that history is written and religions are founded (Seroussi, 2014).

The idea of the Temple is powerful, whether as a symbol of secular Israeli national identity, of Jewish sovereignty, or of evangelical redemption. As I have illustrated throughout this article, the tangible representation of the idea of the Temple is its well-known image established at the Holyland Model. I conclude that the miniature models representing the Temple building\object, and the gigantic buildings representing the Temple model \thing, continuously interact to produce both imagined and concrete subject-object relations and meaning.

Notes

1. For a detailed analysis of this model, see Padan (2017a).
2. See for example Abramson (2006); Amit (2009); Avi-Yonah (1966); Cohen Hattab and Kerber (2004); Tsafrir (2009).
3. For a detailed analysis of this model, see Padan (2017b).
4. For example: The Hebrew Music Museum, The Temple Institute, the Mikdash Educational Center.
5. A non-profit educational and religious organization that promotes the building of the Third Temple instead of the Mosques on the Temple Mount:

   > Our short-term goal is to rekindle the flame of the Holy Temple in the hearts of mankind through education. Our long-term goal is to do all in our limited power to bring about the building of the Holy Temple in our time. Temple Institute website: https://www.templeinstitute.org.

Disclosure statement

No potential conflict of interest was reported by the author.

References

Abascal, I. M. (2014). Translating sacred architecture: Solomon's temple in Sao Paulo. *The Avery Review*, no. 4.

Abramson, L. (2006). A pile of things. In L. Abramson (Ed.), *"Mini Israel", 70 models, 45 artists, one space* (pp. 148–156). Jerusalem: The Israel Museum.

Amit, D. (2009). *Model of Jerusalem in the second temple period*. Jerusalem: The Israel Museum & Holyland Tourism (1992) Ltd.

Avi-Yonah, M. (1966). *A short guidebook to the model of Jerusalem from the end of the second temple period*. Jerusalem: Holyland Corporation.

Balakirsky Katz, M. (2011). Avi Yonah's model of second temple Jerusalem and the development of Israeli visual culture. In S. Fine (Ed.), *The temple of Jerusalem: From Moses to the Messiah* (pp. 349–364). Leiden: Brill.

Be'er, Y. (2013). Dangerous Liaison: The dynamics of the rise of the temple movements and their implications. (Report). Retrieved from Ir Amim website: http://www.ir-amim.org.il/en

Black, M. (1962). *Models and metaphors: Studies in language and philosophy*. Ithaca, New York: Cornell University Press.

Brabant, M. (2001, February 5). Jewish Fury at the 'holy land' park. *BBC News*. Retrieved from http://news.bbc.co.uk

Branham, J. R. (2008). The temple that won't quit: Constructing sacred space in Orlando's holy land experience theme park. *Harvard Divinity Bulletin*, 18–31.

Brown, B. (2001). Thing theory. *Critical Inquiry*, *28*(1), 1–22.

Bruckner, D. (2010, November 19). A dream coming true. *Makor Rishon, Shabbat Magazine* (Hebrew). Retrieved from https://musaf-shabbat.com

Casanova, J. (2001). Religion, the new millennium, and globalization. *Sociology of Religion*, *62*(4), 415–441.

Cherni, H., & Tsafrir, Y. (2009). Creators of the model. In D. Amit (Ed.), *Model of Jerusalem in the second temple period* (pp. 14–16). Jerusalem: The Israel Museum & Holyland Tourism (1992) Ltd.

Cohen Hattab, K., & Kerber, J. (2004). Literature, cultural identity and the limits of authenticity: A composite approach. *International Journal of Tourism Research*, *6*, 57–73.

Cohen-Hattab, K., & Shoval, N. (2015). *Tourism, religion and pilgrimage in Jerusalem*. London: Routledge.

Culler, J. (1988). *Framing the sign: Criticism and its institutions*. Oxford: Basil Blackwell.

Lavie, Z. (1964 November 20). Built Jerusalem. *Maariv*, p. 35.

Liebman, C. S., & Don-Yehiya, E. (1983). *Civil religion in Israel: Traditional Judaism and political culture in the Jewish state*. Berkeley, CA: University of California Press.

Long, B. O. (2003). *Imagining the holy land: Maps, models and fantasy travels*. Bloomington, IN: Indiana University Press.

MacCannell, D. (1976). *The tourist: A new theory of the leisure class*. New York, NY: Schocken Books.

Morrison, T. (2013). The built narrative as architectural history. *The International Journal of Literary Humanities*, 10(1), 1–18.

Padan, Y. (2017a). *Modelscapes of nationalism: Collective memories and future visions*. Amsterdam: Amsterdam University Press.

Padan, Y. (2017b). Moving the second temple. In N. Hazan (Ed.), *The mount, the dome and the gaze: The temple mount in Israeli visual culture* (pp. 91–99). Tel Aviv: Tel Aviv University.

Persico, T. (2017). The end point of Zionism: Ethnocentrism and the temple mount. *Israel Studies Review*, 32(1), 104–122.

Philips, T. (2010, July 21). Solomon's temple in Brazil would put Christ the redeemer in the shade. *The Guardian*. Retrieved from https://www.theguardian.com

Reiter, Y. (2001). Holiness and politics in the temple mount's history. In Y. Reiter (Ed.), *Sovereignty of god and man: Sanctity and political centrality on the temple mount* (pp. 5–20). Jerusalem: The Jerusalem Institute for Israel Studies.

Ribon, N. (1965, April 2). Next year – Jerusalem is built. *Haaretz*, p. 24.

Romero, S. (2014, July 24). Temple in Brazil appeals to a surge in evangelicals. *New York Times*. Retrieved from https://www.nytimes.com

Seroussi, B. (2014). Inferno. In 31ª Bienal de São Paulo, Guia da exposição [31st Biennale of Sao Paulo, Exhibition Guide]. English translation. Retrieved from http://www.bienal.org.br/texto.php?i=1136

Silberman, N. A. (2001). If I forget thee, O Jerusalem: Archaeology, religious commemorations and nationalism in a disputed city, 1801–2001. *Nations and Nationalism*, 7(4), 487–504.

Simmons, S. (2010, August 31). New Aish Center at the western wall. Retrieved from Aish HaTorah website: http://www.aish.com/ci/s/78061807.html

Spalding, J. (2002 July 3-10). Authentic Replica. *Christian Century*, p. 14.

Stevenson, J. (2013). *Sensational devotion: Evangelical performance in twenty- first-century America*. Ann Arbor, MI: The University of Michigan Press.

Stewart, S. (1993). *On longing: Narratives of the miniature, the gigantic, the souvenir, the collection*. Baltimore, MD: The Johns Hopkins University Press.

Tsafrir, Y. (2009). Introduction. In Amit, D. *Model of Jerusalem in the second temple period* (pp. 9–13). Jerusalem: The Israel Museum & Holyland Tourism (1992) Ltd.

Tuan, Y. F. (1976). Geopiety: A theme in man's attachment to nature and to place. In D. Lowenthal & M. Bowden (Eds.), *Geographies of the mind* (pp. 11–39). New York, NY: Oxford University Press.

Usborne, D. (2001, February 5). Jewish protesters to picket 'holy land' rival to Disney theme park. *The Independent*. Retrieved from https://www.independent.co.uk

Watts, J. (2014, October 1). Brazil's evangelicals become a political force to be reckoned with. *The Guardian*. Retrieved from https://www.theguardian.com

Wharton, A. J. (2006). *Selling Jerusalem: Relics, replicas, theme parks*. Chicago, IL: The University of Chicago Press.

The Musée de la Grande Guerre du Pays de Meaux – a simulacrum of the 1914–1918 war?

Bertram M. Gordon

ABSTRACT

On 11 November 2011, 93 years after the armistice that ended World War I, President Nicolas Sarkozy officially helped open the Musée de la Grande Guerre in Meaux, near the bloody Marne River battle sites of 1914 and 1918, as well as near Disneyland Paris. The new museum included a reconstituted battlefield with a 'no man's land' plus three-dimensional projections to 'revive the hell of a trench.' Speaking at its groundbreaking in 2010, Frédéric Mitterrand, then Minister of Culture and Communications, stated that the museum's architecture of the trenches would produce an intimate memory, conveying real flesh and blood. He added that it would also 'reinforce the cultural and tourist appeal' of the Marne region. A crowning recognition of Jean-Pierre Verney's amassing of some 50,000 documents and objects relating to the war, which forms the basis of its collection, the museum has welcomed more than 460,000 visitors since it opened. Philippe Dagen suggested in Le Monde in 2011 that the high quality of the exhibitions and the attention to detail might distract visitors' attention from the true horror of the war. Edward Rothstein, a New York Times reporter, wrote: 'the real focus of the museum was not on the military or the political issues, but on the personal.' In this essay, I maintain that the museum, with its re-created landscapes of battlefield tourism is, by its nature, a simulacrum or simulacre, defined in both English and French as an illusion, or something possessing the form or appearance of a certain thing, without possessing its substance or proper qualities (Oxford English Dictionary and Trésor de la Langue Française). Having visited the museum in 2012, I focus on how it presents its architectural simulacra of trenches and battleground landscapes to its twenty-first-century visitors, including the many groups of school children who form an important niche tourism audience. I also argue that, despite arguments sometimes made that denigrate simulacra as somehow shallow and inauthentic, the simulacra of a museum such as that at Meaux, attempting to highlight the horrors of war, serve desirable ends and are thus to be supported. Although displaying artifacts from many nations, the Meaux museum is very much an icon of France's national heritage honoring its wartime soldiers and civilians. Its very creation there as a way to keep Verney's collection in France is a significant part of this narrative of national heritage.

The Musée de la Grande Guerre, or the Meaux Museum, raises interesting and important questions of simulacra and memory because the intent of its founders was clearly to recreate in the minds of its visitors the feeling of the horrors of World War I's trench warfare in northeastern France. This article accordingly addresses the history of the Museum, established in the town of Meaux in the outer suburbs of Paris.[1] The account of the Museum's history is followed by consideration of whether such an institution can be anything other than a simulacrum or *simulacre,* defined in both English and French as an illusion, or something possessing the form or appearance of a certain thing, without possessing its substance or proper qualities.

The variations of a word – simulacra

The *Oxford English Dictionary* [OED] traces the use of the term 'simulacrum' as referring to 'a material image, made as a representation of some deity, person, or thing' to the late sixteenth century. Its more current meaning in the OED is 'something having merely the form or appearance of a certain thing, without possessing its substance or proper qualities,' a usage cited in the *Edinburgh Review* in 1805. French language practice parallels that of the English. The *Trésor de la Langue Française* offers an older meaning of 'the representation of a deity.' Its primary definition, however, is given as a 'figurative image or representation of something concrete' [*Image ou représentation figurée d'une chose concrète*] used by Victor Hugo in his *Choses vues* in 1885. In both English and French, the more neutral definitions are not alone in usage of the term. English and French definitions include negative or pejorative usages as in the case of the English 'a mere image, a specious imitation or likeness, of something' and the French 'false appearance, illusion, phantom, false pretense. A simulacrum of government, judgment, peace, power' [*Fausse apparence, illusion. Synon. fantôme, faux-semblant. Un simulacre de gouvernement, de jugement, de paix, de pouvoir*] (Oxford English Dictionary, n.d. and Trésor de la Langue Française, n.d.). An example of simulacra in the world of tourism may be seen in Little World, 'one of many foreign "theme parks,"' where, in the words of Nelson Graburn, who has studied it, Japanese tourists create their own 'authenticity.' A museum, Little World 'consists of more than twenty-five "authentic" foreign villages, compounds, hacienda etc. built along a road winding 3 + km. through the rolling countryside north of Nagoya' (2017).

Despite the sometimes negative connotations of the term 'simulacrum' in the writings of Jean Baudrillard and others, the reality of simulacra may be desirable or undesirable depending on the ends to which they are put. The creation of such tourist simulacra, in other words, if they help sensitize their visitors to the horrors of war, may in the end be something to be valued. Indeed, the Meaux Museum works to help educate its audience, in large measure groups of school children brought there in organized group visits, to gain a greater understanding and appreciation of the horrors of First World War trench warfare. Created within the past decade, the Museum has a relatively brief history.

A Museum to highlight the horrors of war – a visual and auditory experience

On 11 November 2011, ninety-three years after the armistice that ended the First World War, French President Nicolas Sarkozy officially helped open the Musée de la Grande

Figure 1. Source for map: https://www.worldatlas.com/webimage/countrys/europe/frenchregions/friledefrance.htm. Every effort has been made to contact the copyright holders.

Guerre in Meaux, near the sites of the bloody battles of 1914 and 1918, along the Marne River. As shown in the map below, the museum is located in the eastern Paris suburbs, some fifty-five kilometers east of the city and approximately twenty kilometers from Disneyland Paris, although the lack of direct public transportation from Paris may have subsequently depressed the numbers of visitors (Figure 1).

Designed to send an antiwar message to its visitors, the Musée de la Grande Guerre recreates architectural micro-environments such as representations of trenches and battleground landscapes to its twenty-first century visitors, including the many groups of school children who form an important niche audience. The exhibits include the reconstruction of a battlefield, along with airplanes and tanks of the war years. There are, however, limits in the battlefield reconstructions. For example, although visitors may see and hear the sights and sounds of battle, they cannot smell the battlefield, nor can they actually physically enter a trench for the feel of the battle experience, both reminders of the near impossibility of recreating the full sensory experience of past events (Figure 2).

As vivid as the war scenes represented in the display cases are, for example, there is no reproduction of the smells of battle.[2] The Museum relies instead on visual and auditory

Figure 2. A display case showing simulated soldiers, Musée de la Grande Guerre at Meaux.

sense experiences with film and sound projections, and multimedia terminals that may be touched and manipulated by visitors (Giansily, n.d.). Exhibits include a reconstituted battlefield with a 'no man's land' plus three-dimensional projections to 'revive the hell of a trench' (Mitterrand, 2010) (Figure 3).

The Museum was built near the American Monument, *La Liberté éplorée* [The Tearful Liberty], a statue dedicated to the Americans who fought in France during the First World War. Sculpted by Frederick MacMonnies, and erected in 1932, the American Monument was paid for by subscriptions from more than four million American citizens. The statue was erected on the exact spot where the German offensive on the Marne had been halted in September 1914 (Waymarking, 2011). In December 2016, two statues of Marshal Joseph Gallieni, who had played a key role in the French victory at the Marne in 1914, were moved to the Museum. Both were the work of the sculptor Eugène Benêt, whose statue of the victorious French soldier [*Poilu victorieux*] of the First World War, has been reproduced widely in France. One of the two Gallieni statues, in plaster, dated to 1920, was placed inside the Museum. The second, a bronze replica, had been installed in 1923 in Trilbardou in the Seine-et-Marne Department, where it had been the object of an attempted theft in 2007. It was placed subsequently on the grounds outside the Museum (Marchand, 2015).

Preserving France's heritage and promoting tourism

In large measure, the Museum project was conceived and promulgated by Jean-François Copé, Deputy-Mayor of Meaux as a way of acquiring historian Jean-Pierre Verney's

Figure 3. A reconstituted trench with a film of First World War soldiers, The Musée de la Grande Guerre at Meaux.

collection of some 50,000 documents and objects relating to the war, which forms the basis of its holdings. Verney had put his collection up for sale and there was a possibility that it would be bought by an American purchaser and moved out of France. Wishing to promote local tourism, Copé also saw in the Museum project a 'locomotive for the north of the department' (Le musée vivant de la mémoire, 2007). Although displaying artifacts from many nations, the Museum is very much an icon of France's national heritage honoring its wartime soldiers and civilians. The reconstruction of history and wartime heritage presented in the Meaux Museum becomes an iconic guide to nationality including the efforts to keep Verney's collection in France as a significant part of this narrative of national heritage.

This essay is based in part on a day spent at the Museum on 22 June 2012 with the late Anthony Joseph 'Tony' Bianco, Jr., an American friend then visiting Paris. The Museum, a contemporary-style building constructed from concrete, glass, and metal, is described on the Museum's web site as 'a site of today to speak of yesterday.' The web site continues:

> Set in natural slope of the land, in a horizontal position that speaks to the verticality of the American monument, the building offers many viewing points, enhanced by pedestrian pathways from the roof and the forecourt, creating a permanent dialogue between them.[3] (Le plus grande musée de l'Europe 14–18, n.d.)

A large angular contemporary-style structure above a smaller glass-enclosed ground floor reception area, the Museum forms an esthetic contrast with the *Liberté éplorée,* sculpted in the more traditional style of interwar memorials (Figure 4).

Because the reception area is so much smaller than the main structure above, one enters beneath the main structure through a shaded area evoking the darker emotions of the war. Its collection includes military uniforms, postal cards, weapons, newspapers, medical instruments, a variety of objects made by the French soldiers in their trenches, and everyday items such as soldiers' dining utensils. Life size figures of the soldiers in uniform, together with an officer on horseback, add to the realistic qualities of the exhibits, which also show the transition from red to a more subdued blue military tone for the French soldiers' trousers, following the carnage of 1914. Included are posters relating to the work of animals during the war and a German poster from the occupied town of Chauny ordering the killing of all carrier and domestic pigeons. Photos of French colonial soldiers are also exhibited. Lastly, television monitors show clips from the interwar years,

Figure 4. The Musée de la Grande Guerre at Meaux with the statue *La Liberté éplorée* nearby.

including film of British Prime Minister Neville Chamberlain following his return from Munich in 1938, highlighting the failure to achieve peace after the First World War.

Originally planned to be five thousand square meters in surface, the Meaux Museum, was twice the size of the Historial de Péronne, near the First World War Somme battlefields. No fewer than 45,000 items related to the war were brought together in its collection (Le musée vivant de la mémoire, 2007). As of August 2018, the Museum claimed more than 65,000 objects and documents, its web site noting that it was the largest museum in Europe dedicated to the First World War. Its building, designed by the architect Christophe Lab, is constructed in concrete, glass, and metal, and described in the web site as 'deliberately contemporary [*volontairement contemporain*].' It is, the web site continues, 'a place of knowledge, discovery, and pedagogy.' The Museum is now 7000 square meters in size, of which 3000 hold the permanent exhibition, 'integrating into its structure the presentation of iconic pieces: the domes for aircraft, the pit for the tank, and the space for the reconstruction of the battlefield' (Le Musée de la Grande Guerre Pays de Meaux, n.d.). The battlefield reconstruction is that of a trench in real-life dimensions, some 100–150 meters in length.

'A full vision of the conflict' and an 'Intimate memory'

In contrast to the Historial de Péronne, near the site of the Battle of the Somme, the Meaux Museum was designed to show 'a full vision of the conflict, evoking life in the rear, the role of women, and medical progress,' according to Michel Rouger, who headed the project while still underway in 2007, and served as Director of the Museum through 2016 (Abjean, 2016). It was to include material from the 1917 mutinies and items related to the roles of soldiers from the French colonies. Rouger saw the Meaux Museum as complementing the more 'intellectual' character of the older Péronne Historial. The Meaux Museum's approach was to be 'more feeling than intellectual,' according to Rouger, and to attract a clientele that seldom visited museums. Key to the Museum was to be the 100–150 meter long reconstructed trench, the 'highlight' [*clou*] of the exhibition, to use Rouger's word (Le musée vivant de la mémoire, 2007).

While many war museums and monuments offer a kind of 'top down' public perspective, creating constructions of memory focusing on the role of the state and political action in producing the trauma of war, the Meaux Museum is oriented more toward a view from the 'bottom,' more specifically the more private experiences of the soldiers in the trenches and the civilians who endured wartime privation (Confino, 1997, p. 1395). In its focus on the private histories of the war, frequently overlooked in the emphasis on the state and the political by public monuments and museums, the Museum, given its location at an important battle site, also seeks to evoke a sense of place or what Nancy Wood refers to as a 'symbolic topography' (Wood, 1999, p. 3).

Speaking at its groundbreaking in 2010, Frédéric Mitterrand, then Minister of Culture and Communications, stated that the Museum's architecture of the trenches would produce an intimate memory, conveying real flesh and blood. The economics of tourism also played a role as Mitterrand added that it would also 'reinforce the cultural and tourist appeal' of the Marne region (Mitterrand, 2010). From its opening in 2011 through 2015, some 532,000 visitors toured the Museum, with a peak of 133,333 in 2014, the centennial anniversary of the war and the first Battle of the Marne (Le musée de la Grande Guerre, 2016). The numbers fell in 2015 in part because of heightened secur-ity measures regarding school trips following attacks in France that year, which contribu-ted to a twenty percent decline in visits by school groups. In 2015, fifty-three percent of the visitors came as individuals, thirty-seven percent in school groups, and ten percent in adult groups. Some fifty percent visited from the Ile-de-France region, of whom half were from the department Seine-et-Marne, and three percent from Paris. The relatively low pro-portion of visitors from Paris has been explained in part by the need to take at least one train and bus to access the Museum from the city and possibly more, depending on one's point of origin in Paris. Forty-five percent of the visitors came from Britain, America, Belgium, the Netherlands, and other foreign countries (Fréquentation Musée de la Grande Guerre du Pays de Meaux en 2015, 2016).

Philippe Dagen suggested in *Le Monde* in 2011 that the high quality of the exhibitions and the attention to detail might distract visitors' attention from the true horror of the war (Dagen, 2011). Edward Rothstein, a *New York Times* reporter, echoing Rouger's thought, wrote: 'the real focus of the museum was not on the military or the political issues, but on the personal' (Rothstein, 2011). The Museum contains a wide variety of objects, includ-ing multimedia and digitized items in an effort to enable the visitor to comprehend the war as well as acquire a sense of the changes affecting the societies at war in the early twentieth century.

The simulacrum of a First World war soldier – 'Louis Vivien's' Facebook page

In 2013, Rouger participated in the creation of a Facebook page for 'Louis Vivien,' a fictional First World War *poilu*, or soldier, based on photographs from the Meaux Museum's collection. The Facebook page was to be an extension of the Museum's work. Again, Rouger maintained that the goal was to offer a 'human' dimension of the war to the largest possible audience. Louis Vivien was to have been a teacher [*instituteur*] who could offer a critical perspective on the war and 'show it in all its absurdity' (Les invités du 36e, 2013). Verney participated in the project, which focused on the years 1914 and 1915, so that the character Vivien would not have known how long the war would last. Discussing the Facebook page in words that echoed his view of the Museum, Rouger explained:

> The project's goal was to 'highlight our collections and make them alive. In addition, how does one approach so many of the themes that we wished to address: camaraderie, life and death in the trenches, the fear, etc.? And then, how could one allow oneself to use an authentic tes-timony to "invent" a woman, a mother, friends, etc.?' (Les invités du 36e, 2013)

Asked about the fact that simulating soldiers' wartime letters was rendered all the more difficult as they had been censored during the war, Rouger replied that the idea of the Facebook page was to imagine a soldier with a smartphone in the trenches in 1914 com-municating with his fellow soldiers on their Facebook pages. More than 54,000 people fol-lowed the Louis Vivien Facebook page, which ran for one month and a half, intentionally kept short for lack of resources to keep it running but also to maintain a feeling of the tension of the events and to preclude boredom on the part of the viewers. Rouger told of viewers who had never previously opened a book about the First World War but who had eagerly anticipated the updated Facebook pages. The project would be used subsequently for school children (Les invités du 36e, 2013).

The news of the death of Louis Vivien on the battlefield in 1915, transmitted via Facebook a century later evoked messages of sympathy and requests for a published book that could be 'used by teachers in class,' or as a souvenir for those who wished to remember (Voilà déjà, 2013). An article by Aude Deraedt in the newspaper *Libération* reported that 'the *poilus* are not dead, they still tweet.' Noting that as of November 2012 Louis Vivien was the first World War I soldier to have a social media page in France, Deraedt quoted Rouger who emphasized the rigor with which the Museum staff had written the Louis Vivien Facebook posts. Others in France have since followed the Louis Vivien model, including regular posts on Twitter based on diaries kept by real soldiers during the war and now in the possession of their descendants. In one case, *Libération* reported that the Second World War Mémorial de Caen in Normandy had created a fictional American soldier, Louis Castel, who tweeted an account of the Allied landings there seventy years after D-Day (Deraedt, 2014).

The war Museum, the internet, and simulacra

With the Louis Vivien project, the Musée de la Grande Guerre is clearly in today's world of virtuality as well as simulacra. In yet another layer of simulacra, the museum may be toured virtually as well. A Twitter post in January 2018 showed a classroom of middle school (3ème du collège) students viewing the Musée de la Grande Guerre from their classroom in Brittany (Cornillet, 2018). A museum of war by its very nature with its re-created landscapes of battlefield tourism will be a simulacrum, and the example of a fictitious soldier with twenty-first century technology transported back a century earlier exemplifies Baudrillard's comments in his essay *Simulacra and Simulation* where he differentiates between representation, in which something real is portrayed, and simulation, a model of something real that ultimately becomes a simulacrum, a creation defined only by itself with no basis in reality. Representation, in Baudrillard's words, is the 'equivalence of the sign and the real,' whereas simulation is 'the principle of equivalence, *from the radical negation of the sign as value,* from the sign as the reversion and death sentence of every reference' (Baudrillard, 1994, p. 6).

Addressing museums specifically, Dean MacCannell differentiated between those that focused on 'collections' in contrast to those that were devoted more to 're-presentations.' A re-presentation, he wrote, 'is an arrangement of objects in a reconstruction of a total situation.' Re-presentation, he argued, inevitably involved some element of intervention on the part of those organizing the display. It 'aims to provide the viewer with an authentic copy of a total situation that is supposed to be meaningful from the standpoint of the things inside of the display.' MacCannell associated 're-presentations' with natural history museums, as they sought to recreate a setting in the wild, and 'collections' with art museums that gathered paintings and other artworks without attempting to place them into a larger narrative (MacCannell, 1976, pp. 78–80). A similar argument might be made also for war museums, which also use their objects to tell a story. It might even be suggested that the human impulse for war, after all, is itself a part of the natural world.

The Meaux Museum is one of many war museums that convey narratives or in various ways attempt to tell the stories of the many wars in the history of France dating back to

Roman times.[4] Compared to other First World War museums in France, such as that at Péronne and the museum in the the Verdun Memorial, the Meaux Museum may be said to be oriented more toward an emotional than intellectual understanding of the war, although this is difficult to measure. The museum at Verdun, established in 1967 by Maurice Genevoix, a veteran of the 1916 battle and author, later elected to the Académie Française, closed in 2013 but reopened on 21 February 2016 to commemorate the centennial of the battle. As its web site stated in 2018, the passing of the last survivors of the Battle of Verdun, together with the coming of new generations, made it necessary to 'recast the museography' [*refondre la muséographie*] in order to reach new audiences. 'The new scenography,' according to its web site, 'which combines pedagogy and emotion, plunges the visitors into the heart of the Great War and the Franco-German battlefield' (Genèse d'une Renaissance, n.d.).

It has been suggested that in the presentation of its displays the Meaux Museum 'looks just like any other museum,' highlighting the difficulty faced by all museums in transmitting the full effect of their contents to the public.[5] This suggestion reflects the fact that the reality of war may be presented only through the representations or, if one prefers, the simulacra of tourism architecture, such as the reconstructed trenches and battleground landscapes.

Yet another step away from the actual battlefield representation may be seen in the landscape immediately surrounding the Musée de la Grande Guerre. The hills around the Museum retain their wartime geographic perspectives but the immediate landscape and its uses have changed. As evocative as the American Monument, *La Liberté éplorée*, may be to the visitor, it is a postwar addition and thus a step away from representing the war itself. Its emotional impact in contrast to that of a pristinely preserved battlefield may be debated. The use of the grounds, however, continues to evolve. A news account in April 2018 reported a group practicing Pilates exercises in the Museum's garden and suggested that it might be difficult to see a connection between stretching exercises and the 1914–1918 war, although it added that Joseph Pilates, for whom the exercises are named, lived in Great Britain and developed his regimen during the war (Meaux, 3 September 2017). The varied activities in and around the Museum appear to have been successful as the numbers of visitors showed an eighteen percent increase in the summer of 2017 over the figures for the previous year (Meaux, 14 September 2017). Plans were underway to commemorate the centennial of the 1918 Armistice at the Museum with President Emmanuel Macron and some eighty additional heads of state to be invited (La Marne, 2018).

Conclusion: are simulacra necessarily problematic?

Discussing what he saw as a postmodernist focus on the indifference of tourists to simulations and simulacra, Arthur Asa Berger noted that visitors to the Taj Mahal very much wish to know that what they are seeing is 'the real thing and not an imitation' (Berger, 2013, p. 33). Not all cases, however, are as clear as that of the Taj Mahal. As Stéphanie Nkoghe writes, tourists in general receive a wide variety of stimuli and in effect 'see, hear, touch, taste' creating an experience stored in their memories. A tourist's memory includes information from before, during, and after travel (Nkoghe, 2008, p. 55). Tourists visiting museums that in some form attempt to recreate the past must of necessity be seeing some kind of re-creation, or what Baudrillard calls 'simulacrum.' Nkoghe's comment, however, raises the question of whether memory itself should be considered as simulacrum. To at least some extent all memory itself is a simulacrum, a re-creation, or to use MacCannell's term, a 're-presentation,' of the past in the brain of a present living human.

In the case of the Meaux Museum, the attempt to simulate the sense of war inevitably involved interventions on the part of the curators even if many of the objects themselves, such as boots and weapons, were the real items used during the war. A similar dichotomy exists between the 'authentic' and 'inauthentic,' in which case it might be suggested that the boots and weapons exhibited in the Meaux Museum are authentic, even if the scenes using them in the display are not.

Rather than a strict dichotomy, however, there is a range between representation and simulation and the objects and presentations in museums such as that at Meaux all fall somewhere along this range. The objects, such as weapons or other items used during the war, may be real but an effort to recreate a sense of the war experience may be a rep-resentation or simulacrum, again using Baudrillard's dualism, depending on the degree that they reflect some demonstrable reality connected to the conflict. The difficulty lies in sorting out what is demonstrable reality and what is not, especially as one visitor's reality may not be the same as the next. The very vocabulary of simulacra and authenticity tends to assume clear distinctions that are apparent to all but may itself be an expression of unexpressed value judgments.

It is difficult to imagine any representation of war, produced by a museum or otherwise, being other than in some form a representation or simulacrum unless the visitor is actually watching war unfold, such as the spectators who witnessed the battle of Waterloo, the tourists gazing at battles during the 1853–1854 Crimean War,[6] or those who watched the military action at the first Battle of Bull Run (Manassas) during the American Civil War of 1861–1865 (King, 2004, p. 32). Even eyewitnesses of war may give very differing accounts of their experiences from those represented in the Meaux Museum, as in the case of Mary Seacole describing the excitement she felt while watching the Tchernaya battle during the Crimean War and her 'longing to see more' (Seacole, 1988, pp. 147 and 169). Writing about observers watching the fighting in Gaza in 2014, Jan Mieszkowski noted retrospectively that

> At the beginning of the nineteenth century, warfare came to be understood as a theatrical performance, a clash of armies that should respect the unity of time and place as if it were a classical drama. (Mieszkowski, 2014)

If, in fact, war may be understood at least in part as theatrical performance or classical drama, this is hardly a product of the nineteenth century. Homer's *Iliad* and *Odyssey* come immediately to mind and one may ask how different the simulacra and virtualities of the twenty-first century are from the romantic sagas and representations of earlier times. Rouger suggested that many who followed the Louis Vivien Facebook page had never before read any history of the war, although it should be noted that schoolchildren in France learn about the war and many have heard family stories about it, although in declining numbers as the last World War I veterans in France have passed on in recent years. The key for Rouger and his team was less to make today's visitors familiar with the principal events of the war than to stimulate their interest in it, to make it come alive for them, hence the simulacra. Their project serves as a reminder that even war, as

dramatic as it may seem, may be perceived as boring and uninteresting to later generations and that the task of pedagogy, for adults as well as for children, is to enhance
the audience's interest in the subject. The *Iliad* and *Odyssey* are commonly taught as historical sources, complete with the awareness that much of their content may never be fully
verified historically. Again, a significant part of the Meaux Museum's mission is pedagogi-
cal, teaching about war to the many school children who visit in groups. As early as 1801, a
governmental report under Napoleon Bonaparte emphasized the role of museums in educating students through narratives for patriotism and the glory of the fatherland (Poulet,
2005, p. 161). While the Meaux Museum is oriented more toward peace than the glorifica-
tion of war, it tells a story and in its preservation of the Verney collection, seeks to enhance
a sense of national heritage among its visitors.

   With all the frequently discussed issues of commodification and kitsch in tourism and
museums, one must wonder if the mission of the Meaux Museum, stated as educating its
visitors about the horrors of war, can be presented other than with simulations and simulacra. Discussing 'dark tourism' to scenes of death and tragedy, Peter E. Tarlow asks: 'In our
desires to preserve the tragedies of the past are we creating an artificial world?' 'Few
people,' he continues, 'would want to experience the fog of war first hand; almost no
one would willingly suffer the torment or death of a concentration camp nor run for
one's life from the collapsing Twin Towers,' an allusion to the attacks of 11 September
2001 in the United States. Most people, he argued would want the 'simulata' rather
than live the real experience (Tarlow, 2005, p. 52). Perhaps the changes made to appeal
to its twenty-first century audience, while in many cases simulacra moving away from Baudrillard's sense of representation, are able to reach the Museum's visitors more viscerally
than the more representational forms that Baudrillard seems to prefer. To be sure, the
Meaux Museum represents a form of tourism architecture as a mode of storytelling, presenting a point of view and seeing history through its own lens. The very creation of the
Museum as a way to keep Verney's collection in France is part of a narrative of national
heritage.

   Addressing Baudrillard's conception of simulation, Steven Best and Douglas Kellner
wrote:

> Simulation for Baudrillard thus describes a process of replacing 'real' with 'virtual' or simulated
> events, as when electronic or digitized images, signs, or spectacles replace 'real life' and
> objects in the real world. Simulation models generate simulacra, representations of the real,
> that are so omnipresent that it is henceforth impossible to distinguish the real from simulacra.
> The world of simulacra for Baudrillard is precisely a postmodern world of signs without depth,
> origins, or referent. (Best & Kellner, 1997, p. 101)

Much that is in the Meaux Museum, and the affiliated Facebook page of Louis Vivien,
especially, might seem to conform to Baudrillard's critique of a 'postmodern world of
signs without depth, origins, or referent.' It might be argued, however, that the fictional
Louis Vivien character does not fall within Baudrillard's category of simulacra or simulation
as no effort was made to pretend that Vivien was a real life person. The clearly articulated
purpose of the Museum, however, and its open discussion of the fiction involved in creating the Louis Vivien Facebook page make clear the referent and, in many ways encourage
the virtual tourists to investigate further for themselves. Differences between real soldiers'
diaries posted on digital social media a century later and the fictional account of Louis

Vivien, no matter how carefully crafted and how well-intentioned, posted there again highlight the need for a spectrum or a grid rather than a dichotomy in analyzing a range from representation through simulation to hyper-reality, again using Baudrillard's terminology. A museum will always be in some way a simulacrum of what it represents. On the other hand, there are different layers of representation relating in different ways to simulacra. Contemporary paintings of battlefields or display cases showing weapons of the war, such as at Meaux, are not simulacra. They are in fact the real items. However, the representations of the battle or the war itself, must of necessity be simulacra, given the impossibility to recreate the actual event with its actual participants. That there are tourist sites, perhaps in the order of Disneyland, that conform more to Baudrillard's critique of simulacra is evident. The *Musée de la Grande Guerre du Pays de Meaux* clearly is not one of them.

Notes

1. This chapter is a revised version of the paper, 'Architecture and Tourism: The Musée de la Grande Guerre du Pays de Meaux - A Simulacrum of the 1914–1918 War?' presented at the Architecture and Tourism, Fictions, Simulacra, Virtualities Conference in Paris in July 2017. It has been re-written to take into account comments made at the conference and subsequently together with the author's additional reflections on the issues of simulacra and memory as they relate to architecture and tourism.
2. My thanks to Nelson Graburn, who in a reading of an earlier draft of this essay, asked whether the Museum reproduced the smells of the battlefield, thereby suggesting some of the limitations in the attempts to reproduce the experience of warfare.
3. The original French text reads: 'S'inscrivant dans la pente naturelle du terrain, dans une horizontalité qui répond à la verticalité du monument américain, le bâtiment offre de nombreux points de vue, renforcés par des liaisons piétonnes depuis le toit et le parvis, créant ainsi un dialogue permanent entre eux.'
4. For a fuller discussion of tourism, aesthetics, and war, see the Introduction in my book, *War Tourism: Second World War France from Defeat and Occupation to the Creation of Heritage* (Ithaca, NY: Cornell University Press, 2018).
5. Comment following my presentation, Architecture and Tourism, Fictions, Simulacra, Virtualities Conference, Paris, 6 July 2017.
6. During the Crimean War, British tourists viewed the Tchernaya battle and the bombardment of Sebastopol from the surrounding Crimean hills. Mary Seacole's description of the excitement she felt while watching the battle and her 'longing to see more' has become well-known to students of war reportage. Her work was published. See Seacole (1988, pp. 147 and 169).

Disclosure statement

No potential conflict of interest was reported by the author.

References

Abjean, G. (2016, July 9). Des adieux émouvants au directeur du Musée de la Grande Guerre. *La Marne*. Retrieved from https://actu.fr/ile-de-france/meaux_77284/des-adieux-emouvants-au-directeur-du-musee-de-la-grande-guerre_8473861.html

Baudrillard, J. (1994). *Simulacra and simulation*. Translated by Sheila Faria Glaser. Ann Arbor: University of Michigan Press.

Berger, A. (2013). *Theorizing tourism: Analyzing iconic destinations*. Walnut Creek, CA: Left Coast Press.

Best, S., & Kellner, D. (1997). *The postmodern turn (critical perspectives)*. New York, NY: The Guilford Press.

Confino, A. (1997, December). Collective memory and cultural history: Problems of method. *American Historical Review*, *102*(5), 1386–1404. Addresses the distinction between public and private memory in war memorials.

Cornillet, G. (2018, January). Mardi après-midi … . *Twitter post @cig_FMargot*. Retrieved from https://twitter.com/search?q=musée%20de%20meaux&src=typd&lang=en

Dagen, P. (2011, November 11). La Grande Guerre s'expose à Meaux, sans sang, sans cris, sans larmes. *Le Monde*. Retrieved from http://www.lemonde.fr/culture/article/2011/11/10/la-grande-guerre-s-expose-a-meaux-sans-sang-sans-cris-sans-larmes_1601931_3246.html#xtor%3dEPR-32280229-[NLTitresdujour]-20111111-[titres]

Deraedt, A. (2014, August 4). Les poilus ne sont pas morts, ils tweetent encore. *Libération*. Retrieved from http://www.liberation.fr/ecrans/2014/08/04/les-poilus-ne-sont-pas-morts-ils-twittent-encore_1075373

Fréquentation Musée de la Grande Guerre du Pays de Meaux en 2015. (2016, October 16). Musée de la Grande Guerre du Pays de Meaux, Accueil Portail 77 Actualités Tourisme Sorties Vie, La-Seine-et-Marne.com. Retrieved from http://www.la-seine-etmarne.com/actualites/frequentation-musee-de-la-grande-guerre/

Genèse d'une Renaissance. (n.d.). *Mémorial de Verdun Champ de Bataille*. Retrieved from http://memorial-verdun.fr/museecollections/le-musee/genese-et-renaissance

Giansily, H. *Musée de la Grande Guerre du Pays de Meaux*. Retrieved from http://france.fr/fr/a-decouvrir/musee-grande-guerre-pays-meaux

Graburn, N. (2017). *Rittoro Wārudo – Little World: Too Much Authenticity for Playful Japanese Tourists*. Abstract, paper presented at the Architecture and Tourism, Fictions, Simulacra, Virtualities Conference, Paris, July; and at the The Tourism Studies Working Group seminar, University of California, Berkeley, September. Retrieved from http://www.tourismstudies.org/news_archive/Graburn2017.htm

King, C. (2004, April 23). *Laws and wards of war*. Review of Clive Ponting, The Crimean War, Times Literary Supplement.

La Marne. (2018, January 18). *80 chefs d'Etat attendus au musée de la Grande Guerre*. Actu.fr/La Marne. Retrieved from https://actu.fr/ile-de-france/meaux_77284/80-chefs-detat-attendus-musee-grande-guerre_15131191.html

Le musée de la Grande Guerre, 5 ans et plus de 500 000 visiteurs. (2016, November 11). *Le Parisien*. Retrieved from http://www.leparisien.fr/espace-premium/seine-et-marne-77/le-musee-de-la-grande-guerre-5-ans-et-plus-de-500-000-visiteurs-11-11-2016-6314112.php

Le Musée de la Grande Guerre Pays de Meaux/Le Plus Grande Musée d'Europe 14–18. (n.d.). Retrieved from https://www.museedelagrandeguerre.eu/fr/visiter-le-musee/le-plus-grand-d-europe-sur-14-18.html

Le musée vivant de la mémoire. (2007, November 8). *Le Point*. Retrieved from http://www.lepoint.fr/actualites-region/2007-11-08/le-musee-vivant-de-la-memoire/1556/0/209241#

Le plus grande musée de l'Europe 14–18. (n.d.). *Musée de la Grande Guerre, Pays de Meaux*. Retrieved from http://www.museedelagrandeguerre.eu/en/visiter-le-musee/le-plus-grand-d-europe-sur-14-18.html

Les invités du 36e: Michel Rouger et Léon Vivien. L'homme de Meaux et l'homme de mots. (2013). Le 36e RI: des Normands dans la Grande Guerre, 21 mai 2013. Retrieved from http://36ri.blogspot.com/2013/05/les-invites-du-36e-michel-rouger-et.html

MacCannell, D. (1976). *The tourist : A new theory of the Leisure class*. New York, NY: Schocken Books.

Marchand, J. C. (2015, December). *Statue Gallieni s'installe au Musée*. Le Portail La Seine&Marne.com. Retrieved from https://www.la-seine-et-marne.com/actualites/statue-gallieni-sinstalle-musee/

Meaux: le musé e de la Grande Guerre remonte aux origines du « Pilates. (2017, September 3). *Le Parisien*. Retrieved from http://www.leparisien.fr/meaux-77100/meaux-le-musee-de-la-grande-guerre-remonte-aux-origines-du-pilates-03-09-2017-7232304.php#xtor=AD-1481423554

Meaux: près de 20% de visiteurs en plus cet été au musée de la Grande Guerre. (2017, September 14). *Le Parisien*. Retrieved from http://www.leparisien.fr/meaux-77100/meaux-pres-de-20-de-visiteurs-en-plus-cet-ete-au-musee-de-la-grande-guerre-14-09-2017-7260789.php#xtor=AD-1481423553

Mieszkowski, J. (2014, July 18). War, with popcorn. *The Chronicle of Higher Education*. Retrieved from http://chronicle.com/blogs/conversation/2014/07/18/watching-war/?cid=wb&utm_source=wb&utm_ …

Mitterrand, F. (2010, April). Discours de Frédéric Mitterrand, ministre de la Culture et de la Communication, prononcé à l'occasion de la pose de la première pierre du Musée de la Grande Guerre de Meaux. Retrieved from http://www.culture.gouv.fr/mcc/Espace-Presse/Discours/Discours-de-Frederic-Mitterrand-ministre-de-la-Culture-et-de-la-Communication-prononce-a-l-occasion-de-la-pose-de-la-premiere-pierre-du-Musee-de-la-Grande-Guerre-de-Meaux

Nkoghe, S. (2008). *La Psychologie du Tourisme*. Paris: L'Harmattan.

Oxford English Dictionary. (n.d.). Retrieved from http://www.oed.com.intra.mills.edu:2048/view/Entry/180000?redirectedFrom=simulacrum#eid

Poulet, D. (2005). *Une histoire des musées de France, XVIIIe-XXe siècle*. Paris: La Découverte/Poche.

Rothstein, E. (2011, 11 November). Bringing the war home. *New York Times*. Retrieved from http://www.nytimes.com/2011/11/12/arts/design/museum-of-the-great-war-opens-in-meaux-france.html?scp=2&sq=edward+rothstein&st=nyt

Seacole, M. (1988). *Wonderful adventures of Mrs. Seacole in many lands*. New York, NY: Oxford University.

Tarlow, P. E. (2005). Dark tourism: The appealing 'dark' side of tourism and more. In M. Novelli (Ed.), *Niche tourism: Contemporary issues, trends and cases* (pp. 47–58). Amsterdam: Elsevier.

Trésor de la Langue Française. (n.d.). Retrieved from http://stella.atilf.fr/Dendien/scripts/tlfiv5/advanced.exe?8;s=3509506860

Voilà déjà six mois que Léon est tombé. (2013, November 28). In *Louis Vivien*, Facebook. Retrieved from https://www.facebook.com/leon1914/

Waymarking. (2011). *Le Monument Americain – Meaux, France – World War I Memorials and Monuments on Waymarking.com*. Retrieved from http://www.waymarking.com/waymarks/WMB0YN_Le_Monument_Americain_Meaux_France

Wood, N. (1999). *Vectors of memory: Legacies of trauma in postwar Europe*. Oxford: Berg.

Simulacra architecture in relation to tourism: Charles Rennie Mackintosh in Glasgow and Antoni Gaudi in Barcelona

Yasmin Buchrieser

ABSTRACT

An increasing global competition between cities encourages many of them to find ways to promote and develop a unique identity and increase their attractiveness as a tourist destination. Some cities may develop and promote an emblematic architect and his or her architectural heritage/legacy, like the examples of Glasgow and Charles Rennie Mackintosh and Barcelona and Antonio Gaudi. Furthermore, this article will focus on the way tourism can lead local actors in cities to go even further and to continue to build their architecture, even after the death of the architects. A phenomenon appears where architecture is posthumously continuing to be built, leading to the production and creation of simulacra and facsimiles (for example of Mackintosh architecture in Glasgow and Gaudi architecture in Barcelona) for tourist, commercial and heritage reasons. This article aims to present and discuss how architectural heritage can be produced and transformed 'for' and 'by' tourism, a fascinating change in these cities which has also been the subject of criticism and leads to many questions.

1. Introduction

Today, in a globalized world, and an increasing competition between cities (Pumain, 2001; Prisching, 2011, p. 86), many seek to find ways to distinguish themselves, and local actors try to develop the city's uniqueness as a tourist destination (Gravari-Barbas, 2013, p. 23). To succeed, cities may use different strategies, such as singularization (Biau, 1992) and building a strong urban identity (Galland, 1993), place branding (Ashworth, 2009) and/or urban development through culture (Evans, 2003), a strategy that has been used by several post-industrial cities like Barcelona, Glasgow or Bilbao (Gomez, 1998; Rodrigues-Malta, 1999; Rodríguez Morató, 2005). In this respect, one of the most-known strategies cities may use are the creation of an iconic structure like the Guggenheim Museum in Bilbao (Plaza, 2006), the organization of mega-events like the European Capital of Culture in Glasgow in 1990 (García, 2005; Mooney, 2004), or the branding of an existing local cultural heritage, like for example a specific and emblematic local architecture and architect (Ashworth, 2010; Gravari-Barbas, 2004, 2007). This article focuses particularly on cities that have chosen to build their urban development and tourism strategy on architecture (Buchrieser,

2017; Gravari-Barbas, 2007) and analyzes the phenomenon of reconstructing and produ-cing architecture even after the death of the architects.

The examples of Barcelona and Glasgow are interesting due to the architectural recon-structions. In both cities, posthumous constructions of Gaudi and Mackintosh architecture exist and are built mainly in the city where their construction had initially been started or had been planned to be built. Similar examples are the reconstructions of the works of Frank Lloyd Wright, among others (Levine, 2008). Levine explains that these types of reconstructions of the past became more and more numerous during approximately the last thirty years (Levine, 2008).

The examples of reconstructed architecture existing in Glasgow and Barcelona are different compared to the simulacra examples in China (Bosker, 2013) or the theme park architecture, which are certainly the most known examples where traditional archi-tecture has been removed and reconstructed in another country or city than its origin. Indeed, entire villages, like the Austrian alpine village Hallstatt, or Venice with the canals or Paris with the Eiffel Tower have been reconstructed as copies or simulacra, principally in China as Bosker states: *'Entire townships and villages appear to have been airlifted from their historical and geographical foundations in England, France, Greece, US, and Canada and spot welded to the margins of Chinese cities'* (Bosker, 2013, p. 3).

Theme parks like 'Disneyland' or others like 'Little World' in Japan use themed and simu-lacra architecture. Hence, in 'Little World' in Japan, 24 'villages' have been built by import-ing or simulating exactly different styles of traditional architecture of countries from five continents (Graburn, 2004; 2017). Simulacra architecture has also been used in Las Vegas, which tends to resemble a theme park (Gravari-Barbas, 2001), where typical and iconic architecture of famous cities has been rebuilt. In Las Vegas, it is possible to visit Par-isian monuments like the Eiffel Tower or the Arc de Triomphe, to admire the Pyramids of the Hotel Luxor, or to ride gondolas on Venetian canals and visit St Marcus square.

This article specifically focuses on reconstructed works of famous architects, usually in the city of origin or in the city where the architect had planned to build this project. Here, the style and the identity of an architect, of an icon and his works are reconstructed, as opposed to the reconstructed architecture in China or in theme parks, where often build-ings that represent a tradition, a country, a culture, and less the work of the architect himself, even if this architect is also associated to his city are represented.

Instead, cities like Barcelona and Glasgow have started to make heritage in their cities using an existing architectural heritage. In the case of Mackintosh and Gaudi's architectural heritage a growing trend of producing, creating and recreating, and even reinterpreting and artificially transforming the original heritage and its image has been observed. The architectural heritage serves as a tool for promoting the city, and at the same time, tourism and visitors who are interested in this heritage play a driving role in the desire to continue to rebuild and even produce new heritage in the same architectural style.

These two examples are particularly revealing because the cities did not only valorize, preserve and promote their existing architectural capital, but they went even further and developed and increased this initial capital. These cities will go beyond the limits of crea-tivity, using architectural styles in the most diverse or unexpected fields, calling upon certain know-how and awareness of profitability and attractiveness of this singular archi-tectural heritage. Finally, the question of the limits arises. What are the limits and the con-sequences of this tendency to rebuild and produce architectural heritage many years after an architect's death? How does this transform or influence the image of these architects and their heritage?

Two case studies, Gaudi in Barcelona and Mackintosh in Glasgow will be analyzed and the reproduction and the reconstruction of their architectural heritage will be discussed.

2. Production and reconstruction of Mackintosh architecture in Glasgow

Interestingly, a part of the Mackintosh-related attractions or heritage in Glasgow is partially reconstructed copies of the architect's authentic designs, facsimiles or simulacra. In addition, we observe that rebuilt Mackintosh themed architecture begins to develop more and more in Glasgow. Among different cities strongly associated to an architect, Glasgow is certainly one that has the strongest tendency to posthumously reconstruct the works of an architect.

We recall that the architectural heritage built by Mackintosh, is a key attraction of the city, which distinguishes itself by its singularity and originality, and represents a unique cultural resource for Glasgow that is known as an industrial, working-class city. We also observed that both, the heritage initially built by the architect and the posthumously reproduced copies, attract visitors. In Glasgow, the proportion of Mackintosh themed architectural copies is high compared to other cities.

The case of Mackintosh and Glasgow is specific, thus we analyzed in detail how this reconstructed architecture appeared and developed in Glasgow. Thereby we observed that this is a quite recent phenomenon. Indeed, this recreated Mackintosh heritage has not always existed in Glasgow and has been built only in the last 30 years by local actors. Interestingly, this trend continues as new copies or reconstructions of Mackintosh's architecture and design are built in Glasgow.

It is important to understand why and how local actors in Glasgow made the decision to create simulacra and facsimiles of Mackintosh's works and that tourism is a factor that plays a role in their production. What impact do simulacra and facsimiles have on the heritage of the architect? To understand and analyze Mackintosh's case, we will focus on two examples of Mackintosh-related works that have been subject to partial or total transformations and reconstructions.

2.1. The example of house for an Art Lover: a simulacrum built as an 'Interpretation of Mackintosh'

House for an Art Lover is very interesting, because its plan and the initial drawings had been designed by Mackintosh, but he finally never built it, but it was brought to life years after his death. Mackintosh created drawings in 1901 in collaboration with his wife Margaret MacDonald, for a competition launched by a German magazine to build a 'House for an Art Lover'. However, as he did not win the competition this house was not built. Only, in 1987, sixty years after Mackintosh's death, Graham Roxburgh, a consulting engineer, discovered these drawings and had the idea to build this house in Glasgow. He thought: *'Here was a project of European dimension, yet with a uniquely Glaswegian identity, matching a present day window of opportunity'* (Roxburgh, 2006, p. 30). This project became reality a few years later and the house opened in 1996 in Glasgow's Bellahouston Park (Figure 1).

Figure 1. House for an Art Lover, an 'interpretation' of Mackintosh. (a) House for an Art Lover from the exterior. (b) Signboard indicating when the house was 'designed' and when it was 'built'. Sources: (a) and (b) Yasmin Buchrieser (August 2010).

Mackintosh's drawings were used as a source of inspiration and a basic model for detailed building plans adapted to the challenge of constructing the house that existed only on paper. House for an Art Lover is seen as an 'Interpretation of Mackintosh', and not as an exact replica of Mackintosh's design. In addition, Mackintosh's original function for the house – that was the home of an art lover – had been changed. Indeed, as the property manager explains *'Graham Roxburgh's plan for the House for an Art Lover was for it to become a visitor center, so people could come'*.[1] Thus, Roxburgh's idea was to build the house for commercial and tourist purposes and not residential ones, as Mackintosh's original plan. To adapt the house to these new functions, elements of the original Mackintosh project had been changed or removed, and new elements had been added, as the property manager explains:

> We don't see ourselves as a Mackintosh building, this is almost as a research project [...] Mackintosh did the drawings, they were incomplete, and Graham built the drawings around Mackintosh's designs [...] and the house was always going to be a visitor center, there was always going to be office accommodation, and that was the reason why they actually sneaked an extra floor into the house, and that helps us with the commercial viability of the business.[2]

Thus, the priority of the House for an Art Lover construction was not to accurately reconstruct Mackintosh's designs, but to use them in the way that suits their business project.

Thus, the House for an Art Lover built in 1996 can be seen as a simulacrum of the house drawn by Mackintosh in 1901, with modifications and the integration of elements from other Mackintosh works. For example, elements of the Hill House or the Mackintosh Church at Queens Cross served as a model for recreating missing elements in Mackintosh's drawings (Roxburgh, 2006, p. 37). Hence, House for an Art Lover in Bellahouston Park is a creation that has never existed exactly as such, not even on Mackintosh's drawings. As Levine explains, the constant need to adapt to conditions and requirements that change over time, results in changes in the form and function of the original design and presents the biggest obstacle to authenticity for a posthumously constructed building (Levine, 2008).

The manager explains the position of this house in relation to the original Mackintosh buildings:

> 'I think people come for both reasons. I think people come to the house and think we're actually the real thing, they think that Mackintosh built the house, and that he was alive when the house came to life, and there are people that come along knowing that it's an interpretation of Mackintosh's competition entry, and Margaret MacDonald of course.'[3]

Building the house has been criticized on a number of occasions. Academic scholars tend to say that it is not comparable to the works Mackintosh built himself, but today it is solidly integrated and actively participates in the groups that work to preserve and promote Mackintosh in Glasgow, as the property manager explains:

> I think initially there was some skepticism about the house, whether it should have been built, or shouldn't have been built, but the fact is, it was built. It's here, it's functioning, it's part of the actual Mackintosh offer, and I think you know, most people in the Mackintosh world have accepted the House for an Art Lover for what it is, really.[4]

Thus Mackintosh's brand and architecture had been used because the architect's work had the ability to attract visitors. 'I think in that particular point, there was research done that Glasgow probably attracted 200,000 people a year to come and see Mackintosh, and the house was built in order to try and capitalize in that.'[5] The house is a product created to be consumed by visitors and tourism and commercial activity and about £ 40,000 a year are spent on marketing.[6]

If tourism and visitors initially had an important place, the house turned more and more towards commercial activities, such as the organization of events like weddings, which became the principal activity as it generates important benefits, necessary for a self-financing company: *'We absolutely have no income funding at all.* [...] *So everything that we generate, we're self-sufficient.'* [7] As it has given the priority to events it is often closed for visitors on weekends, and visitor numbers have dropped. However, events have become an important activity for museum-houses worldwide, as it is an efficient way to generate significant profit and enabled museum-houses to become self-financing. Today the event market partly finances the preservation and maintenance of heritage.

The link with Mackintosh allows House for an Art Lover to differentiate itself and to benefit from the promotion that is made of the architect in the city. Its future projects are to continue to develop the house, the commercial activity and events, as well as the creation of a heritage center, including a part on Mackintosh. The long-term project is to transform Bellahouston Park into Glasgow's Art Park. To conclude, House of an Art Lover is a simulacrum that, on the one hand, takes advantage of Mackintosh's architecture and brand, and at the same time works to encourage and develop heritage, art, and culture in Glasgow.

2.2. The example of the Willow tea rooms: developing a brand

During his career, Mackintosh designed four tea rooms[8] in Glasgow, commissioned by Mrs. Cranston. In 1918, she sold all her tearooms, including those designed by Mackintosh. Today only the Willow Tea Rooms, located on Sauchiehall Street is preserved as such.

To briefly recall the context, in the 1980s, a woman had the idea to rent the second floor of the original Willow Tea Room building, to recreate Mackintosh's tearooms. The idea was *'bringing it [the tea room] back to the way that it was in 1904 until 1928.'*[9] Some elements Mackintosh designed had been preserved, and others had been destroyed and had thus to be recreated, as the owner explains:

> the Room Deluxe was empty, the panels were all still here, so they are original, and they are there since 1903, and the doors are original. Downstairs there is a lot of reconstruction. But there are still original pieces throughout the building. The gallery was reconstructed. [10]

The 'Room Deluxe' was inaugurated in 1983, following the big success of the tea room, she progressively rented other spaces of the building and continued to rebuild the interior of the Willow Tea Rooms. In 2013, she took over the entire building.

At the time these tea rooms were reopened, Mackintosh was still relatively unknown in Glasgow, and his work not very accessible to visitors:

> … We had the Garden Festival in December 1988, and lots of people came to Glasgow for the Garden Festival, and we were really busy, and that was why, because they were coming to the city, they'd heard about the Tea Rooms, so then it became a visitor attraction, so it was more than just a tea room.[11]

This example illustrates that elements of Mackintosh' heritage have been recreated and used for commercial and tourism purposes. Indeed, Mackintosh and his unique and distinctive style allowed this tearoom to become unique and attractive to visitors. Today it has become 'more than a tea room', it has become a 'visitor attraction'. Due to the success, the owner continued to develop her Mackintosh brand themed tea rooms and created a second one, a simulacrum. As the owner patented the name 'The Willow Tea Rooms' which became her own brand image, she has the possibility and the right to use these names associated with Mackintosh. Thus, the second tea room she opened in 1997 on Buchanan street, is also called 'The Willow Tea Rooms' (Figure 2), as she explains:

Figure 2. 'The Willow Tea Rooms' on Sauchiehall Street and Buchanan Street, Glasgow. (a) The Willow Tea Rooms on Sauchiehall Street, the original Mackintosh building. (b) The Willow Tea Rooms' reconstructed as a simulacrum on Buchanan Street. Sources: (a) and (b) Yasmin Buchrieser (October, 2014).

'So because I had the Willow Tea Rooms here, we called that the Willow Tea Rooms down there. You know so that the people would identify both tea rooms. […] And it was just to keep that brand.'[12]

The Willow Tea Rooms on Buchanan Street is an example of a creation that never existed. This simulacrum (Figure 3) is composed of several elements inspired by different original Mackintosh tea rooms that were put together or mixed in a new tea room, which:

- is located next door to the building where the original Buchanan Street Tea Rooms designed by Mackintosh had been.
- is called The Willow Tea Rooms, a name originally given to another tea room designed by Mackintosh.
- contains two recreated iconic rooms (the 'Chinese Room' or 'Blue Room', and 'The Ladies' Luncheon Room' or 'White Room') (Figure 3), inspired from The Ingram Street Tea Rooms, a third tearoom, designed by Mackintosh.

This example is fascinating as it shows how this owner started to produce Mackintosh heritage for commercial and tourist purposes. A unique heritage was transformed into a serial product, suggesting that it is possible to create more of them. Indeed, the owner has started a 'Mackintosh themed tea house chain'. These series of tea rooms inspired by Mackintosh's work also transform Mackintosh's image. On the one hand, they help to promote Mackintosh and his work, but as they are reconstructions, they do not project the authentic image. This is criticized or qualified by some as 'Mockintosh', devaluating the work of the architect or giving it a 'too' commercial image.

Furthermore, the owner may go even further in the simulacrum, as this excerpt shows:

If there was to be a third tea room, you know, would we just start it over and call it Mrs Cranston the next time? And just take different bits from different places? Which would be quite interesting as well … [13]

Here, the owner is progressively moving away from the original work of Mackintosh, and it will be interesting to question how these reinvented tea rooms will be identified with

Figure 3. Creation of a simulacrum: 'The Willow Tea Rooms' on Buchanan Street. (a) Reconstruction of 'The Ladies' Luncheon Room' or 'White Room'. (b) Reconstruction of the 'Chinese Room' or 'Blue Room'. Sources: (a) and (b) Yasmin Buchrieser (October 2014).

Mackintosh's original work. The owner comments on this point: *'Oh, still keeping different layers of Mackintosh in it, you know the funny chairs, some medals, you know taking some bits and pieces and putting that back in again […], if you have something more … […]it makes it more interesting.'*[14] Through the idea of introducing iconic or distinctive Mackintosh themed elements, the teahouse owner is in a certain way taking possession of- and benefiting from Mackintosh's brand image to attract visitors and for her commercial activity. Here, we can therefore question the limits.

This question of the limits is even more relevant since the owner of the tea room received a proposal in 1997–2000 to open a Mackintosh Tea Room in Japan:

> And we were approached by people from Japan to see if we would open up a tea room there, they wanted a Willow Tea Rooms there, but it would not have been practical because I had small children at the time. [...] at that time it didn't work. Also, because we started the 'Willow pink products' here, like our tea caddys, we started doing different things.[15]

The project in Japan was not carried through, but the possibility existed, and if themed Mackintosh architecture could have been built in Japan, it could also have been built in other countries. Mackintosh's work has potential and opening a The Willow Tea Rooms in Japan would have certainly contributed to the promotion of Mackintosh abroad.

In 2014, the Irish company that owned The Willow Tea Rooms put the building up for sale. It was bought by a trust, The Willow Tea Rooms Trust, for £ 400,000.[16] Its project is to restore the tea rooms and opening them again as active tea rooms but focusing on the heritage, instead of commercial functions. It also involves the creation of an interactive visitor center with an exhibition, learning and education space, conference facilities and a boutique.[17] Once restored, the tea room will be called 'Miss Cranston's New Tea and Lunch Rooms'.

On June 22, 2016, the trust closed the building for restoration works. The reopening is planned for 2018 to commemorate the 150th anniversary of the birth of Mackintosh. Once finished, the building will be given to the city of Glasgow where it should be self-financed by the profits and funds generated by the trust.[18] It should be beneficial for the development of tourism, and for the city: *'The tea rooms are a catalyst for the regenerof of this part of Glasgow and will become a focal point for Cultural Tourism, attracting both domestic and international visitors.'*[19] More than 150,000 visits are expected and more than 50,000 for the visitor center. [20] Thus, in Glasgow the original Mackintosh tea room will be restored with precision and scientific rigor, and will include reconstructed elements, which will be facsimiles of originals that aim to protect heritage and tourism

The former owner and her 'The Willow Tea Rooms' left the building when it closed for the restoration work, and her tea room was relocated to a department store on the same street (121 Sauchiehall Street), called Watt Brothers.[21] The new Willow Tea Rooms at Watt Brothers opened on September 23, 2016 on the third floor of the department store.[22] Thus, a new simulacrum was added to the Mackintosh teahouse series, which no longer have any direct connection to the original Mackintosh heritage. The posthumously created Willow Tea Rooms, which are simulacra inspired by the architecture of Mackintosh, gradually move away from the original architect's work and are used for commercial activity.

To conclude on Glasgow, the city is an example of how some local actors began to create and produce Mackintosh heritage simulacra in the city, primarily for commercial and touristic reasons. Nevertheless, a desire to respect and value this reproduced heritage is observed, as well as the desire to contribute to raise awareness about the Scottish architect and his work to pass it on to future generations.

Thus, in Glasgow original works built by Mackintosh progressively include reconstructed elements or rooms, which are rigorous facsimiles and whose priority is the protection of heritage and tourism activity. Another example is the reconstruction of the iconic Mackintosh library at the Glasgow School of Art, which was tragically destroyed through a fire in 2014. In contrast, simulacra architecture, such as House for an Art Lover or The Willow Tea Room series was inspired by Mackintosh's work, but does not reproduce it identically and aims commercial and tourist activity. Both, simulacra and facsimiles inspired by Mackintosh's work became attractions for locals and tourists who consume them.

Nevertheless, to preserve the uniqueness and quality of Mackintosh' work, the city and local actors must ensure that his image is not devalued to become 'Mockintosh'. Thus, Glasgow is a fascinating example of a city that preserves, promotes, and restores its architectural heritage, but that has also discovered an innovative way to capitalize on its heritage by reinventing it, recreating it and actually producing new and additional elements of this architectural heritage.

3. Production and reconstruction of Gaudi architecture in Barcelona

As a comparison, we present an analysis of Barcelona and Gaudi. In contrast to Mackintosh and Glasgow, all architectural Gaudi works existing in the Catalan capital were built by the architect himself. However, his most famous work, the Sagrada Familia, is a specific case and exception as it was only partially built by Gaudi himself as he died before he could finish this construction. Gaudi designed the plans of the monumental basilica and built the first part of it, and the construction continued after he died in 1926. Thus, the parts built after Gaudi's death can be seen as a reinterpretation of Gaudi's initial project.

Furthermore, several Gaudi buildings have undergone restoration works, some of which have led to more or less important modifications of architectural elements and have also led to some criticism. For example, the Palau Güell restoration, the progressive alteration of the Park Güell dragon's expression (García-Fuentes, 2016a), or the way the construction work of the Sagrada Familia is carried out (García-Fuentes, 2016b). In addition, Gaudi's tendency to leave his buildings unfinished makes the restoration task more complicated and underlines the difficulty local actors face when building, reconstructing or restoring Gaudi's works (Fuster, 2009). Through these transformations, the Gaudi image shown to tourists today is slowly moving away from the original Gaudi as some details do not always remain faithful to his original work.

Finally, except the continuous construction of the Sagrada Familia, no other Gaudi building has been created by posthumously copying original plans or works of the architect (as observed in Glasgow). However, recently, in Chile, the construction project of a small chapel based on Gaudi's designs has been initiated. This simulacrum will become the first Gaudi building outside Spain.

3.1. The example of the Sagrada Familia

In Barcelona, Gaudi's monumental architectural work, the Sagrada Familia, whose construction is still unfinished (Claveyrolas, 2006), became the city's major tourist attraction.

Its construction is a unique example, as other buildings that Gaudi had left uncompleted like Colonia Güell, have been preserved in the state he left them. Gaudi designed the Sagrada Familia which represented for him 'the work of his life' and dedicated himself to its construction from 1883 until his death in 1926. Since Gaudi's death, his disciples and local actors in Barcelona chose to continue its construction. Thus, over the years, different architects have been in charge of its construction which is planned to be finalized in 2026, for Gaudi's 100th death anniversary.

Today the construction of the Sagrada Familia is financed thanks to the tickets purchased by more than 4,5 million visitors each year (Turisme de Barcelona, 2016), numbers that are increasing rapidly. However, the construction of the Sagrada Familia was not guaranteed in advance, and a regular financial income like today was not always available. At times, the construction was uncertain and threatened, due to a lack of money and the political climate, causing also the loss of valuable construction plans (Descharnes & Prévost, 1982, p. 50). For example, Gaudi's designs of the Passion Façade, unfortunately disappeared during the 1936 civil war (Descharnes & Prévost, 1982), and the façade built today was redesigned. In addition, the Catalan sculptor, Josep Maria Subirachs (1927–2014) created the sculptures for the façade, adding his personal style to the monument. Hence, the Sagrada Familia is no longer 'only' Gaudi design, but visitors also admire the work of Subirachs.

Gaudi himself worked on the Sagrada Família for 43 years, from 1883 to 1926, but from 1926 to its completion planned in 2026, there are 100 years, during which other architects continued its construction. This means that Gaudi has built only part of the final Sagrada Família and the rest is a simulacrum, an interpretation of what is thought that Gaudi might have built. Indeed, we will never know how Gaudi really would have finished the construction of the basilica, as he prepared only a few detailed plans in advance and often improvised (Descharnes & Prévost, 1982, p. 201) as the designs he presented to the authorities or his patrons, rarely revealed his final intentions (Collins, 1960, p. 15). That the part not built by Gaudi is a simulacrum, is also reflected in the inscription on the UNESCO World Heritage List of 'Works of Antoni Gaudí' (UNESCO, 1984) where only 'The Nativity Façade and the Crypt of the Sagrada Família', the part built by Gaudi before his death, are part of the extension of the inscribed property in 2005. This also means that this building, which has become with more than 4,5 million visitors a year (Turisme de Barcelona, 2016) the most visited monument of Barcelona, and even of Spain and that is seen as Gaudi's masterpiece and the icon of the city, is in large part a simulacrum, a reconstruction and a reinterpretation of the design imagined by Gaudi.

However, it is thanks to the strong tourist attraction that the continuous construction of the Sagrada Familia is possible. Indeed, it is self-financing by the entrance tickets purchased and from donations. As the number of visitors has increased strongly in recent years, the construction has also progressed faster. It is a work built 'by' and 'for' tourists, as shown in this excerpt: *'Currently there is so much tourism that of course it is a very high percentage, which enters through tourism. [...] All the money that goes in is to do the construction, so to finish the Temple.'*[23] As an example, we can see the way the Sagrada Familia changed in 10 years (2004–2014) (Figure 4).

This leads us to question of the power of tourism, and finally, if tourism makes 'everything' possible. If you can build such a monument by drawing inspiration from an architect's design, why wouldn't then other unfinished projects be built and materialized as well? What will happen when the Sagrada Família is completed? And, if it represents such a tourist and financial success, and a fascinating project for Barcelona, why would the city not continue, and build another work inspired by the plans of projects Gaudi has left unfinished. Why wouldn't the construction of Colonia Güell also be continued and completed?

3.2. Gaudi is exported internationally: the project of the Gaudi chapel in Chile

For the first time, a work by Gaudi will be completely rebuilt outside Spain. A small chapel whose original plans were designed by Gaudi, will be constructed in the city of Rancagua, in the south of Santiago, Chile's capital. The origin of the project dates back to 1922, when the Franciscan monk Angélico Aranda asked for a 'Portiuncula'[24] for the City of Rancagua', and wrote a letter to Gaudí to ask him for plans: 'I would like to build something original – very original – and I thought of you'.[25] In exchange of the plans, he promised him to pay with prayers. Gaudi accepted because he thought that the requested chapel corresponded perfectly to an edicule (small building), which he had designed for the Sagrada Família and dedicated to the Assumption of Mary. However, the chapel was never built, and the documents of the project remained forgotten for years.

More than 70 years later, these documents were rediscovered, and in 1996 the Corporación Cultural Gaudí de Triana[26] was founded in Chile, to build the Chapel in Rancagua. It is part of a broader project, the creation of a Gaudi Cultural and Spiritual Center of Triana in Rancagua. The original plans designed by Gaudi were used to develop the model of the

Figure 4. Evolution of the Sagrada Familia in 10 years: Nativity Facade built by Gaudi, and construction work in progress. (a) Sagrada Família in 2004. (b) Sagrada Familia in 2014. Sources: (a) Yasmin Buchrieser (November 2004), Yasmin Buchrieser (May 2014).

chapel Nuestra Señora de los Ángeles, which will be a simulacrum or facsimile of the chapel that was planned for the Sagrada Familia. The design of the project was conducted by an architect in 2010 and the professional team formed by Elena Corbalán, Álvaro Guerra and Eugenia Moreno[27] and is supported by the Chilean government. Announcing the costs of more than $ 7 million, Chilean President Michelle Bachelet said she is confident that the center will become a major attraction in the region: *'We are certain that this will be a huge asset for the city of Rancagua.'*[28] The crypt of the Chapel will house the remains of Aranda.[29] Thus twenty years after the initial idea, the cultural corporation Gaudí de Triana will see the project become reality. The construction started beginning of 2016 and the opening to the public is expected end of 2018.[30] This shows how strong Gaudi has become as an international icon and brand, as a center dedicated to him will contribute to the development of a city in Chile.

Through the construction of this chapel, Chile will be the only country in the world, to have a building designed by Gaudi outside Spain. During his life, Gaudi imagined two other projects outside Spain. The Franciscan Missions (1893) for Tangier in Morocco, and a hotel in New York (1909–1910), but neither was built. Thus, if the Sagrada Familia continues to be built in Barcelona, and the project of a chapel designed by Gaudi was rediscovered and will be built years after the death of the Catalan architect, perhaps other Gaudi projects that have not been completed in his lifetime could be built now and produce new simulacra to attract visitors and expand Gaudi's brand throughout the world?

To conclude, in Barcelona, we notice that Gaudi's work is very well preserved. For some time, his buildings were neglected, some of the objects he designed, or furniture were destroyed, nevertheless, comparing with other cities and architects – such as Charles Rennie Mackintosh in Glasgow or Victor Horta in Brussels, where some of their remarkable buildings have been demolished[31] – Gaudi's buildings have yet undergone alterations but none of them has been demolished.

Finally, it seems that a trend to export Gaudi internationally has been initiated. Gaudi has become an icon that is no longer only used by his own country, but also by others who are beginning to use this Catalan icon and are proud to have also a part of Gaudi in their country, like in Chile.

Gaudi has proven to be a strong brand image, very effective in attracting visitors, projects or places that can claim a link with Gaudi. We can question what impact this new place dedicated to Gaudi in Chile will have for tourism in Rancagua? How will the citizens of Rancagua identify themselves with this heritage, which comes from elsewhere? Catalans and international tourists will they go to see the simulacrum of Gaudi in Chile, or will the visitors mostly be local?

4. Conclusion

In this article, a phenomenon that has developed particularly in recent years has been analyzed: the posthumous reconstruction or construction of architect's buildings or their unfinished projects. It was observed that simulacra architecture, an imitated and produced heritage, does not receive the same recognition as the original heritage, which was actually built by the architect during his lifetime. This seems true especially from the perspective of the expert and academic world, and has repeatedly been the object of criticism.

Tourists generally aspire to visit the buildings that were originally built by the architects, however, simulacra architecture also attracts them, and is thus also efficient in terms of tourist and commercial activities. Even if they were not actually built by the architect himself during his lifetime, they allow the visitor to 'live the experience'.

Through this research, tourism was identified as a driving force encouraging the construction of simulacra architecture. It pushes local actors seeking to attract tourism to create and produce more architectural copies. Thus, the example of the Sagrada Familia, which is perhaps the most emblematic, shows that, indeed, it is not only heritage that produces tourism, but tourism also produces heritage (Gravari-Barbas, 2012).

If one can produce a facsimile or simulacrum, wouldn't this suppose that one could produce multiple versions of the same building possibly in different parts of the world? This phenomenon has already begun with the Mackintosh themed tea room chain, which is simulacra of Mackintosh' architecture. If famous enough, this tea room chain might be expanded to different countries. Thus, given these examples, one can question that if the unique works of an architect – whose characteristic is that it represents a local architectural heritage, distinguishing and identifying a place – can be copied, recreated and produced in the whole world would the initial place and work of the architect not lose a part of this specificity and uniqueness which made it valuable in the beginning? What will be the impact on tourism? Will a tourist still come to Glasgow or Barcelona if it is possible to visit a simulacrum of Mackintosh' or Gaudi's work somewhere else closer? Moreover, how will these simulacra be perceived or change the image of the architect and his work? For example, the locals or tourists who will visit the recreated Gaudi chapel in Chile and who have never been to Barcelona, will the image of the simulacrum replace the one of Gaudi's initial work in their minds?

Notes

1. Source: Interview, Manager, The House for an Art Lover, [22.10.2014].
2. Idem.
3. Idem.
4. Idem.
5. Idem.
6. Idem.
7. Idem.
8. The Buchanan Street Tea Rooms (1896–1897): interiors destroyed, the Argyle Street Tea Rooms (1898): interiors destroyed; the Ingram Street Tea Rooms (1900–1911): interiors removed and preserved at the Kelvingrove Museum and Willow Tea Rooms (1903 & 1916); (Billcliffe, 2012) pp. 28–35 and pp. 64–69.
9. Source: Interview, Manager and owner, The Willow Tea Rooms, [23.10.2014].
10. Idem.
11. Idem.
12. Idem.
13. Idem.
14. Idem.
15. Idem.
16. http://www.heraldscotland.com/news/13168439.Willow_tea_rooms_are_bought_by_trust_and_gifted_to_Glasgow/ (01.08.2017).
17. https://www.willowtearoomstrust.org/project/ (01.08.2017).
18. http://www.bbc.com/news/uk-scotland-glasgow-west-28136146 (01.08.2017).

19. https://www.willowtearoomstrust.org/ (01.08.2017).
20. https://www.willowtearoomstrust.org/project/ (01.08.2017).
21. http://www.bbc.com/news/uk-scotland-glasgow-west-36478526 (02.04.2017).
22. http://www.willowtearooms.co.uk/watts-willow-tea-rooms/ (02.04.2017).
23. Source: Interview, Head of archives and documentation, Marketing and Communication, Junta Constructora del Templo de la Sagrada Familia, [15.07.2013].
24. Portiuncula: Small chapel located inside the Basilica of Saint Mary of the Angels, near Assisi in Italy, a sacred place where Saint Francis recognized his vocation in 1208.
25. https://www.theguardian.com/artanddesign/2015/jan/16/antoni-gaudi-spain-chile-our-lady-of-the-angels-chapel-rancagua (08.02.2017).
26. http://www.gaudichile.cl/quienes-somos/ (08.02.2017).
27. http://www.gaudichile.cl/sobre-el-proyecto/ (08.02.2017).
28. https://www.theguardian.com/artanddesign/2015/jan/16/antoni-gaudi-spain-chile-our-lady-of-the-angels-chapel-rancagua (08.02.2017).
29. https://www.theguardian.com/artanddesign/2015/jan/16/antoni-gaudi-spain-chile-our-lady-of-the-angels-chapel-rancagua (08.02.2017).
30. http://eltipografo.cl/2017/01/obras-de-construccion-de-capilla-gaudi-en-rancagua-finalizarian-a-fines-de-2018/ (09.02.2017).
31. Mackintosh's home at 6, Florentine Terrace, demolished in 1963 or some of his tea room interiors; Victor Horta's Hôtel Aubecq demolished in 1949 and his Maison du Peuple demolished in 1965.

Disclosure statement

No potential conflict of interest was reported by the author.

References

Ashworth, G. J. (2009). *The instruments of place branding: How is it done? European Spatial Research and Policy*, 16(1), 9–12.
Ashworth, G. J. (2010). Personality association as an instrument of place branding: Possibilities and pitfalls. In M. Kavaratzis, & G. Ashworth (Eds.), *Towards effective place brand management: Branding European cities and regions* (pp. 222–233). Cheltenham, UK; Northampton, MA: Edward Elgar.
Biau, V. (1992). *L'architecture comme emblème municipal*, Plan Construction et Architecture. Ministère de l'Équipement, du Logement, des Transports et de l'Espace, Paris.
Billcliffe, R. (2012). *Visiting Charles Rennie Mackintosh*. London: Frances Lincoln Ltd. Published in association with Glasgow Mackintosh. 144p.
Bosker, B. (2013). *Original copies: Architectural mimicry in contemporary China*. Honolulu: Hong Kong University Press. 161p.
Buchrieser, Y. (2017). Quand le tourisme construit des cathédrales: patrimonialisation et mise en tourisme de l'architecture d'Antoni Gaudí à Barcelone et de Charles Rennie Mackintosh à Glasgow. Sous la direction de Maria Gravari-Barbas, EIREST EA 7337, Université Paris I Panthéon-Sorbonne. 538p.

Claveyrolas, M. (2006). Le musée d'un lieu saint en chantier, La Sagrada Família entre archives et achèvement virtuel. Le commerce des cultures. *Gradhiva, 4*, 71–83.

Collins, G. R. (1960). *Antonio Gaudi*. New York: George Braziller. 136p.

Descharnes, R., & Prévost, C. (1982). *Gaudi Vision artistique et religieuse*. Lausanne: Edita/Vilo. 245p.

Evans, G. (2003). Hard-branding the cultural city – From Prado to Prada. *International Journal of Urban and Regional Research, 27*(2), 417–440.

Fuster, A. (2009). Gaudí, mythe ou réalité ? *Perspective, 2*, 301–315.

Galland, B. (1993). Les identités urbaines. In *Cultures, sous-cultures et déviances*. Convention romande de 3e cycle de sociologie 2e session Bulle, 24–26 novembre 1993. Avec Michel Bassand. 16p.

García, B. (2005). Deconstructing the city of culture: The long-term cultural legacies of Glasgow 1990. *Urban Studies, 42*(5), 841–868.

García-Fuentes, J.-M. (2016a). *Preservant Gaudí del mite*. ara.cat. Retrieved from http://www.ara.cat/suplements/diumenge/Preservant-Gaudi-del-mite_0_1594040584.html

García-Fuentes, J.-M. (2016b). Reinventing and reshaping Gaudi: From nation and religion to tourism. Architecture, conflict and change in Barcelona's tourist imaginary. In M. Gravari-Barbas, & N. Graburn (Eds.), *Tourism Imaginairies at the Disciplinary Crossroads. Place, Practice, Media* (pp. 289). Abingdon, Oxon: Milton Park; New York: Routledge.

Gomez, M. (1998). Reflective images: The case of urban regeneration in Glasgow and Bilbao. *International Journal of Urban and Regional Research, 22*(1), 106–121.

Graburn, N. (2004). Inhabiting simulacra: The reimagining of environments in Japan. *Traditional Dwellings and Settlements Review, 16*(1), 39.

Graburn, N. (2017). *Rittoro Wārudo* – Little world: Too much authenticity for playful Japanese Tourists. Paper presented at Architecture and Tourism. Fictions, Imaginaries, Simulacra/*Architecture et Tourisme. Fictions, Imaginaires, Simulacres*. Sorbonne-Panthéon 1, Paris 4–7th July.

Gravari-Barbas, M. (2001). La leçon de Las Vegas : le tourisme dans la ville festive / The lesson of Las Vegas : tourism in a festival city. *Géocarrefour, 76*(2), 159–165.

Gravari-Barbas, M. (2004). Patrimonialisation et réaffirmation symbolique du centre-ville du Havre. Rapports entre le jeu des acteurs et la production de l'espace. *Annales de Géographie, 113*(640), 588–611.

Gravari-Barbas, M. (2007). Mémoires d'architecture, mémoire d'architectes. *Ville en construction : projet, regards d'ailleurs, mémoires*. Texte d'introduction, pp. 1–92.

Gravari-Barbas, M. (2013). *Aménager la ville par la culture et le tourisme*. Paris: Editions Le Moniteur. 160p.

Gravari-Barbas, Maria. (2012). Tourisme et patrimoine, le temps des synergies? In Chérif Khaznadar (Ed.), *Le patrimoine, oui, mais quel patrimoine? Internationale de l'imaginaire, No. 27* (pp. 375–399). Paris: Babel.

Levine, N. (2008). Building the unbuilt: Authenticity and the Archive. *Journal of the Society of Architectural Historians, 67*(1), 14–17.

Mooney, G. (2004). Cultural policy as urban transformation? Critical reflections on Glasgow, European city of culture 1990. *Local Economy, 19*(4), 327–340.

Plaza, B. (2006). The return on investment of the Guggenheim museum Bilbao. *International Journal of Urban and Regional Research, 30*, 452–467.

Prisching, M. (2011). Die Kulturhauptstadt als Groß-event. In G. Betz, H. Ronald, & M. Pfadenhauer (Eds.), *Urbane events* (pp. 85–102). Deutschland: VS Verlag für Sozialwissenschaften.

Pumain, D. (2001). Villes, agents et acteurs en géographie. *Revue européenne des sciences sociales, Librarie Droz Geneve, XXXIX*(121), 81–93.

Rodrigues-Malta, R. (1999). Villes d'Espagne en regeneration urbaine. Les exemples de Barcelone, Bilbao et Madrid. *Annales de Géographie, 108*(608), 397–419.

Rodríguez Morató, A. (2005). La reinvención de la política cultural a escala local: el caso de Barcelona. *Sociedade e Estado, 20*(2), 351–376.

Roxburgh, G. (2006). Building the dream. The realisation of Charles Rennie Mackintosh's house for an Art Lover, Printed and published in the UK. 56p.

Turisme de Barcelona. (2016). *Estadisticas de turismo*. Barcelone: ciudad y entorno. Retrieved from http://www.barcelonaturisme.com/uploads/web/estadistiques/2016OTB2.pdf

UNESCO. (1984). Œuvres d'Antoni Gaudí. Retrieved from http://whc.unesco.org/fr/list/320

Index

Page numbers in *italic* refer to figures.

For Product Safety Concerns and Information please contact our
EU representative GPSR@taylorandfrancis.com Taylor & Francis
Verlag GmbH, Kaufingerstraße 24, 80331 München, Germany